Also by Peter Baxter:
Rhodesia: Last Outpost of the British Empire
France in Centrafrique (Africa@War Vol 2)

Co-published in 2011 by:

Helion & Company Limited
26 Willow Road
Solihull
West Midlands
B91 1UE
England
Tel. 0121 705 3393
Fax 0121 711 4075
email: info@helion.co.uk
website: www.helion.co.uk

and

30° South Publishers (Pty) Ltd.
16 Ivy Road
Pinetown 3610
South Africa
email: info@30degreessouth.co.za
website: www.30degreessouth.co.za

Text © Peter Baxter, 2011

Designed & typeset by 30° South Publishers (Pty) Ltd., South Africa
Cover design by 30° South Publishers (Pty) Ltd., South Africa
Printed by Henry Ling Limited, Dorchester, Dorset, UK
ISBN 978-1-907677-38-0

British Library Cataloguing-in-Publication Data
A catalogue record for this book is available from the British Library

CONTENTS

GLOSSARY & ABBREVIATIONS

2IC	second in command
Ack-Ack	name given to anti-aircraft fire, originating during the Second World War
amaNdebele	minority indigenous ethnic/language group, resident in the Matabeleland region of Zimbabwe; an offshoot of the Zulu
Bandeira de Portugal	Portuguese flag
braai	barbeque (Afrikaans)
BSAC	British South Africa Company
BSAP	British South Africa Police
casevac	casualty evacuation
Chindits	a British long-range penetration force active during the Burma campaign of the Second World War
chiShona	language of the Mashona people
CID	Criminal Investigation Department
CIO	Central Intelligence Organization
CO	commanding officer
ComOps	Combined Operations (Headquarters)
cordon sanitaire	a lengthy combined security fence and minefield that was installed along the northeastern and eastern borders of Rhodesia during the 1970s
Détente	South African policy of appeasement/rapprochement with black Africa during the early 1970s
dwala	a domed granite protrusion commonly seen throughout southern Africa; a geologic precursor to a kopje
Exército Português	the Portuguese army
Flechas	lit. 'Arrows', a Portuguese pseudo unit deployed in Mozambique and Angola
FN FAL	Fabrique Nationale Fusil Automatique Léger (infantry assault rifle)
FN MAG	Fabrique Nationale Mitrailleuse d'Appui Général (general-purpose infantry machine gun, or GPMG)
frantan	locally produced variant of napalm; der. frangible tank
Frelimo	Frente de Libertação de Moçambique, Front for the Liberation of Mozambique
frozen area	operational area 'frozen' of normal security force activity in order to allow Selous Scout pseudo units to operate without risk of interception by normal security force units or to in some other way influence events on the ground
gook	pejorative name for members of one or other of the liberation movements; der. Vietnam War
HALO	high altitude low opening (see below) parachuting technique involving high-altitude deployment with low-altitude opening
(Indep) Coy	the Rhodesian security forces distributed school-leaver national servicemen mainly in a number of independent companies of the Rhodesia Regiment; the companies were rebadged later as Rhodesian African Rifles
Information Scandal	a South African political scandal involving the Department of Information
JOC	Joint Operational Centre
Kikuyu	a tribal grouping focused in the central highlands of Kenya
Manicaland	eastern province of Zimbabwe, traditional home of the Manica sub-group of the chiShona language group
Mashona	majority indigenous language group resident in the Mashonaland region of Zimbabwe
Mashonaland	province of Zimbabwe, the traditional home of the Mashona peoples
Matabeleland	province of Zimbabwe, the traditional home of the amaNdebele people
Mau Mau	a tribally specific uprising that occurred in Kenya between the end of the Second World War and the early 1960s miombo signature woodland pattern common to the central plateau of southern Africa and consisting primarily of various Brachystegia species
MNR	Movimento Nacional da Resistência de Moçambique, National Resistance Movement of Mozambique, also Renamo
mopane	a common woodland tree found in the low-lying regions of southern Africa
muti	traditional medicine or witchcraft (chiShona)
Nguni	Large ethnic group indigenous to the southern and southeastern regions of South Africa, comprising the Zulu and Xhosa, among others
OCC	Operations Coordinating Committee
RAR	Rhodesian African Rifles
Renamo	Resistência Nacional Moçambicana, Mozambican National Resistance (Movement) (also MNR)
RhAF	Rhodesian Air Force
RLI	Rhodesian Light Infantry
SAAF	South African Air Force
SAAFA	South African Air Force Association
SADF	South African Defence Force
SAM	surface-to-air missile
SAS	Special Air Service
SB	Special Branch
Shangaan	an Nguni-derived ethnic/language group occupying the Gaza region of Mozambique/Zimbabwe
sharp end	the operational area (slang)
Skuz'apo	idiomatic chiShona epithet applied to the Selous Scouts; der. 'Excuse me here'
SNEB	Société Nouvelle des Etablissements Edgar Brandt, unguided air-to-surface missile
Supers	nickname applied to the Rhodesian C Squadron SAS
terr	terrorist
TTL	Tribal Trust Land
UANC	United African National Council
UDI	Unilateral Declaration of Independence
Unimog	1.5l and 2.5l multi-purpose auto four-wheel drive medium trucks produced by Mercedes-Benz, a division of Daimler AG
white African	a term applied to white residents or citizens of Rhodesia with a particular fluency in native languages, culture and lifestyles and well and a deep familiarity with the natural environment
ZANLA	Zimbabwe African National Liberation Army, ZANU's armed wing
ZANU	Zimbabwe African National Union
ZAPU	Zimbabwe African People's Union
ZIPRA	Zimbabwe People's Revolutionary Army, ZAPU's armed wing

FOREWORD

Frederick Courteney Selous is one of the most fascinating characters of Imperial Africa, and doubtless one of the greatest of the white sons of Rhodesia. Growing up in the country, I was a member of Selous House at Chancellor Junior School in Umtali and grew up, like most youngsters at the time, feeling a kinship with the legacy of this man who had lived his life in the very best traditions of what we represented as a race on the continent.

Selous was one of those historic figures who was more than the mere sum total of his parts. He represented a large part of the Victorian self image. He personified the cult of amateurism, the quest for high adventure and the desire for a better world that underwrote so much of the philanthropic aspect of empire. Perhaps the most potent illustration of the impact he had on the wider British consciousness of the time is the fact that he is the recognized prototype of H. Rider Haggard's fictional character Allan Quartermaine of *King Solomon's Mines* fame. He epitomized to a generation of avid imperial youth the 'Great White Hunter' creed that was a mainstay of so much popular fiction of the period. He was an enduring hero in a world that was already rich with courageous, colourful and energetic characters.

Selous certainly did define a *version* of the Englishman abroad, not in the pattern of Cecil John Rhodes, whose questionable capital adventures brought ignominy upon the Crown and the Foreign Office, and shame on the legacy of colonial Britain. Nor in the style of men such as David Livingstone who entered the field of exploration with the best of intentions but left behind an unmistakeable aura of eccentricity and failure. Selous was a liberal. He was phlegmatic, educated, thoughtful and erudite. As a champion of fair play in race relations in Africa he represented a clique of liberal Fabians in Britain who defined the moral mission of empire. He lived as a self-deprecating man of action, an author, an accomplished naturalist, a traveller, a gentleman philosopher and perhaps the last of the great imperial frontier individualists.

As a military man Selous had no formal training but a great deal of practical experience. His value during the Matabele Rebellion in Rhodesia in 1896 was thanks largely to his skill as a scout and his general fluency with native languages and behaviour. Later, during the First World War, he was refused service in either of the Rhodesian units—the 1st and 2nd Rhodesia Regiments—as a

Frederick Courteney Selous—the inspiration.

consequence of his age of sixty-four. However, he was ultimately able to secure a commission in the 25th Battalion the Royal Fusiliers under which flag he went on to play his part.

His contribution to the East Africa campaign in particular was signature thanks to the fact that he was one of very few whites in the Allied camp intimately familiar with the Tanganyika territory. He contributed to a number of actions before he was killed by a sniper on the Rufiji River on 4 January 1917.

The legacy of a man such as Selous is not easy to define. His influence was felt during his life over a vast swathe of the continent. As an intellectual and scholar it is his body of written work that set him apart, and as a hunter and a conservationist it is perhaps the vast Selous National Park in Tanzania where the most potent statement of his value to Africa has been made.

Selous was an imperialist to the core, and as such he believed passionately in the higher motivations of the British Empire. Where precisely he would stand in the current debate on Africa is hard to imagine, but one can only assume that his contribution would be wise, thoughtful and positive.

Peter Baxter
Oregon, 2011

PRELUDE:
A BRIEF HISTORY OF WAR IN RHODESIA

On a warm September afternoon in 1890 a British South Africa Company (BSAC) police officer, Lieutenant E.C. Tyndale-Biscoe, ran a Union Jack up a temporary flagpole set into the otherwise unremarkable landscape of Mashonaland. Behind him in even ranks stood the assembled BSAC Police. At the conclusion

of the lesson, read by the Reverend Cannon Balfour, an artillery salute sounded that echoed majestically across a new, vast and empty landscape. This sombre ceremony marked the moment that the publically subscribed and commercially underwritten enterprise of Rhodesia opened its doors for business. While this

Raising the flag at Fort Salisbury, 1890.

An artillery troop of the British South Africa Company Police, 1890.

The Anglo-Boer War, 1899. Southern Rhodesian volunteers ride off to do battle.

was underway, and as the few hundred civilian pioneers dispersed into the surrounding countryside, the birth of a long tradition of military adventure in Rhodesia was underway across the eastern horizon.

It is perhaps worth mentioning here that the colony of Southern Rhodesia was born as a commercial enterprise, authorized by Royal Charter and underwritten by the BSAC. The BSAC Police was the first structured militia in the country, organized in the first instance as a defence force against any possible attack on the mobile column by the amaNdebele and only as a secondary consideration as the law-enforcement arm of the company administration and judiciary. The BSAC Police, later shortened to the British South Africa Police, remained the colony's first line of

defence until the establishment of a regular native battalion and a permanent territorial force.

The BSAC was the creation of Victorian financier and imperialist Cecil John Rhodes, a man of enormous wealth and influence in southern Africa and one of the great enigmas of his age. Rhodes was also a man uniquely in step with his times. He arrived in South Africa immediately after the diamond fields of Kimberley had proved their worth but before they had been effectively monopolized. In this hurly-burly of capital adventure his financial brilliance was perfectly placed. Within a few years Rhodes had reconfigured the economic landscape of a young South Africa and amassed a staggering personal fortune. In this regard he was not that different from many others who followed. What rendered him unique was the fact that he was gripped by an almost religious zeal to push outward the limits of British influence in Africa. His personal fortune, his financial acumen and his wide-reaching political influence were all relentlessly deployed to this end.

The fact that Rhodes laid claim to Mashonaland on behalf of the BSAC, as a first significant step toward the amalgamation of Africa, caused the project to have less practical attributes about it than political. The territory was landlocked and almost entirely virgin with attenuated supply and communication lines stretching back over 1,000 miles to the Cape via Kimberley. Thus, once he had secured the territory, Rhodes was immediately faced with the very difficult problem of how to make it pay.

Part of the solution to this lay in securing access to the Indian Ocean. Fort Salisbury was situated 300 miles or so from the port of Beira which, at that time, was one of Portugal's principal maritime hubs and her second largest port on the east coast of Africa. Under the accepted rules of colonial annexation it had long been understood that practical occupation was the first step toward claiming rights over any given territory. Evidence was to be found on the central plateau of Mashonaland, indicating some limited Portuguese mercantile activity in centuries past, but there had been no permanent Portuguese settlements established in Mashonaland since then. Portugal was therefore forced to concede to Rhodes's claim to Mashonaland west of the Sabi River, but staunchly defended her sole right to the territory east of the river, daring Rhodes to stake a contrary claim.

Rhodes was of course not in the least bit impressed by this sort of forlorn diplomatic posturing. He had every intention of claiming the entire east bank of the Sabi River all the way to the eastern seaboard if he could possibly get away with it. As he saw it, with a British railway line linking a British Beira to British Salisbury, and then on to British Bulawayo, the gates to the great British interior would be thrown wide open.

Rhodes's answer was to bend the rules, take what he wanted and hope he could get away with it later. He had a relationship with the British government that had been founded on this sort of behaviour and he had no reason to assume that he could not somehow square the game this time. His opening move was to browbeat a powerful local chief into ceding his territory to the British under the vague

Kaguvi and Nehanda, the spirit mediums who fomented the 1896 Mashona Rebellion, regarded by later generations of black nationalists as the First *Chimurenga*, the First War of Liberation. Kaguvi and Nehanda were hanged for their troubles and went to their graves as martyrs.

A BSAP Maxim gun squad, East Africa, 1914.

threat of arms. This was achieved quite easily, after which the practical matter of enforcement was left to one Major Patrick Forbes supported by a handful of Company troopers. The expected Portuguese response was not long in coming, at which point Forbes adroitly seized and arrested a high-ranking Portuguese military officer from right under the nose of a large and well-provisioned Portuguese military force. The officer was transported back to Portugal care of Her Majesty, arriving in Lisbon some time later to an exaggerated sense of national outrage, fuelled largely by the fact that the Portuguese crown was utterly powerless to respond.

Not so the general population. A subscription was sought to purchase a battleship while a students' militia was raised with the objective of sailing to Portuguese East Africa, or Mozambique, to settle the matter by force. In the meanwhile, Major Forbes, flush with victory, set off with a handful of stout men to seize the port of Beira for Her Majesty. Before too long, however, a jittery company administrator caught wind of the affair and promptly ordered Forbes back to Fort Salisbury, much to the annoyance of Rhodes it might be added.

Forbes left a young police captain by the name of Herman Melville Heyman to garrison the Company claim to Manicaland and keep an eye on the frontier. It was Heyman and a force of less than 50 troopers who met the large student army as, some four or five months later, it finally made its approach to the new borders of Rhodesia. Despite significantly superior numbers, however, and generally better weapons, the fight went the Rhodesians' way and the young Portuguese patriots soon returned to the coast fewer in number and with Manicaland comprehensively lost.

Heyman had in the meanwhile been discreetly contacted by Rhodes who urged him to ignore the politics and do what he could to take Beira. Again a handful of fit and determined men set off overland through the punishing conditions of the coastal plain to deliver Rhodes his prize. This time, however, it was the British

high commissioner at the Cape, Sir Henry Loch, who heard, or at least guessed, what Rhodes was up to. He swiftly dispatched his military secretary to Beira to intercept the determined Rhodesians with the warning that any of Her Majesty's subjects who entered Beira would be shot, backing up his authority with a small Royal Navy flotilla.

Rhodes never did gain a seaport. The relationship between Mozambique and landlocked Rhodesia briefly froze in the aftermath of it all, but thawed soon after as their complementary economies began to generate a mutual economic dependence. Rhodes was never wholly reconciled to the loss of this opportunity that he blamed on the British government, which in turn gave birth to a general tradition among whites in Rhodesia of enmity and suspicion toward Whitehall. Rhodesians never forswore their British heritage; far from it, they contributed more per capita to the defence of Britian than any other colony, but in doing so they were always quick to add it was for king and empire and not the British prime minister and government of the day.

The colony thereafter grew from strength to strength, with military organization, along with civic institutions, tending for a long time to remain in an *ad hoc* condition. The first major bout of internal insecurity was occasioned by the first Matabele War of 1893, and was met through the raising of district volunteer corps. This campaign was a brief and rousing affair, ending in a comprehensive defeat of the warlike but anachronistic amaNdebele nation. The political boundaries of Rhodesia were defined and, with considerable optimism, the tiny white settler community set about constructing a nation.

The twin rebellions of 1896, involving both major tribal groupings of the colony—the amaNdebele and the Mashona, themselves mutually antagonistic—occurred unexpectedly, and was only narrowly suppressed with the intervention of imperial forces. Rhodesian manpower, however, found itself once again deployed in a collection of civilian militias and volunteer brigades characteristic of the frontier riding days of yore. Each of these fought stirring actions, initially for the purpose of bringing those whites isolated in the countryside into the protection of urban

The Rhodesia Native Regiment on the march during the East Africa Campaign of the Great War.

The Rhodesian African Rifles on patrol in the Malayan jungle.

garrisons, and then later to rout and bring to heel the amaNdebele regiments determined to fight to the death in the hills of the Matopos.

In the aftermath of the Matabele War and the twin rebellions the pacification of Rhodesia was for the time being achieved. This was fortunate because immediately afterward a more general and regional war broke out that drew in imperial troops from across the British Empire, and indeed almost amounted to a world war.

The background to the Anglo–Boer War of 1899 was the struggle for the soul of South Africa that had long raged between Briton and Boer. As part of the imperial response to the inevitable outbreak of war, two Rhodesian volunteer regiments were raised. These were the Rhodesia Regiment and the Protectorate Regiment, both of which operated alongside the British South Africa Police in the border regions of the northern Transvaal and Bechuanaland. All three contributed to the Siege of Mafeking and its eventual lifting as well as the iconic Siege of Eland's River.

The Anglo–Boer War ended in 1902, after which both Rhodesian volunteer units were disbanded. The British South Africa Police resumed its role as the agency of both national defence and law enforcement with the territorial force retained as a very loosely configured citizens' militia, badged as the Southern Rhodesian Volunteers. The First World War gave Southern Rhodesia the opportunity to form its first permanent and organized military structure under local command. The Rhodesia Regiment was revived for service in the African theatre when South Africa was charged by the imperial government with the responsibility of occupying South West Africa, at that time still a German-held territory. South Africa had initially been extremely reluctant to consider accepting a specifically Rhodesian unit, offering instead common command and terms of service to any Rhodesian who wished to join the South African army. Few did, however, with most Rhodesians opting for Europe and the quick and ready action of the Western Front.

Matters changed soon after this when a rebellion broke out in South Africa against the Union decision to enter the war on the side of the Allies. Rhodesian manpower suddenly became vital under any badge, and thus the Rhodesia Regiment was reborn. Men rushed to enlist and in due course the 1st Battalion the Rhodesia Regiment was en route to South West Africa as part of the South African occupying force.

The South West African campaign of the First World War was a brilliant military achievement on the part of the young Union of South Africa. For the Rhodesians, however, it was a disappointment. The 1st Battalion was employed almost entirely in a support and garrison role which caused many who had enlisted to regret not joining their countrymen sailing north to fight in Europe. At the end of the campaign the regiment was disbanded with most members opting to do precisely this. However, a second battalion was raised late in 1915 for service in East Africa where a low-level campaign had been underway since the outbreak of war.

The 2nd Battalion the Rhodesia Regiment was somewhat more fortunate inasmuch as it saw no shortage of action. The East Africa campaign emerged as a protracted and exhaustive fight with an entrenched German force that devolved eventually into an agonizing guerrilla war, fought across a spectrum of hostile central African landscapes. It has often been described as a war more against nature and the elements than against a human enemy. The battalion died in early 1917 of absolute depletion. The inability of a small colony with limited white manpower resources to replace losses necessitated the unit being withdrawn from the field in April, before disbandment in October 1917. Those with an un-assuaged appetite to fight once again sought further action in Europe.

The Defence Act of 1926, one of the first significant articles of legislation enacted under the terms of Responsible Government, reversed this situation with a provision for the permanent formation of two white territorial battalions and a cadet force. The act became *de facto* shortly after with the arrival in the colony of Captain Hugo Watson who was seconded from the War Office to help organize Southern Rhodesia's defences along lines that would endure with a minimum of revision until the advent of majority rule in 1980.

The outbreak of the Second World War in 1939 prompted the wide dispersal of Rhodesian volunteer manpower into many diverse imperial regiments and formations. This was thanks largely to a desire to avoid a repetition of events in East Africa that had seen the decimation of 2RR due to its concentrated deployment in a single theatre. A secondary factor was the need for men of calibre to populate the mid-level command structures of a great many other imperial regiments. Rhodesia had always enjoyed a reputation for providing high-quality manpower and it was precisely this that imperial war planners needed. Rhodesians, therefore, fought in every theatre from the north Atlantic to the jungles of Burma, from East Africa to Fortress Europe, tending most often to find their way into the many special force units such as the emerging SAS and the Long Range Desert Group.

The first regular battalion to be formed in the colony was the Rhodesia Native Regiment, precursor to the Rhodesian African Rifles, a unit raised initially for service in East Africa once it had become clear that white infantrymen were simply unable to operate effectively under such difficult climatic conditions. The Rhodesia Regiment became the main territorial force with the 1st Battalion headquartered in Salisbury and the 2nd Battalion in Bulawayo; detached companies were based in Umtali and Gwelo.

The Rhodesia Regiment would eventually field ten battalions, two as part of the Northern Rhodesian contribution to the military formation of the short-lived Federation of Rhodesia and Nyasaland. The Rhodesia Regiment briefly contained an air wing that in due course became the basis of the Royal Rhodesian Air Force.

The first regular white infantry battalion formed in the colony was the Rhodesian Light Infantry, brought into existence in 1961 as a counter-balance to the potentially unreliable regular black units during a period of wide civil unrest in the Federation. This unit was headquartered in Salisbury, and would in due course form the backbone of Rhodesia's counter-insurgency capacity during the 1970s. Rhodesia was also home to a *de facto* squadron of the British Special Air Service in the form of C Squadron (Rhodesian) SAS.

The evolution of orthodox military structures within Rhodesia followed closely the pattern of the British army. Many of Rhodesia's principal commanders were Sandhurst-trained and

> ## IN THE FAR NORTH.
> ### MOVEMENTS OF RHODESIA COLUMN.
> LONDON, December 13.
> The Rhodesia column, under Colonel Plumer, while advancing towards Mafeking, reports having found that Gaberones, a position about 80 miles north of Makeking, had been evacuated by the enemy since December 2.
> The Rhodesian troops repaired the railway in the vicinity.

Mafeking, 1899.

enjoyed considerable fellowship with the British army. The Rhodesian army was initially trained, armed and equipped by the British, and as such, emerged as a truly British army in terms of its structure, traditions and protocols. Even during the period of isolation that Rhodesia suffered as a consequence of the over-hasty decolonization of the 1960s did not sever that link. Rhodesia was excluded from the Cenotaph during the 1966 Armistice commemorations by the then Labour government, an unpopular decree that outraged as many Britons as it did Rhodesians.

Indeed, even in the aftermath of the 1965 UDI, and during the bitter years of war that are the subject of this narrative, the global political animosity that was directed at Rhodesia rarely included foreign soldiers. These, almost to a man, watched on the sidelines with awe and envy as Rhodesia fought one of the most brilliant, dramatic and successful counter-insurgency wars in modern history.

CHAPTER ONE:
THE FORMATION OF THE SELOUS SCOUTS

"It is imperative that a scout should know the history, tradition, religion, social customs, and superstitions of whatever country or people he is called on to work in or among. This is almost as necessary as to know the physical character of the country, its climate and products."
—Frederick Russell Burnham

One of the last British colonial wars to be fought in Africa was the Rhodesian civil war of 1965–1980. This was not fought directly by the British, as had been the case in Kenya, but by a local expatriate community largely of British descent that had declared itself unilaterally independent from the Crown. The decision to

take this almost unprecedented step was informed by the very real fear that Britain was preparing to arbitrarily hand the country over to majority rule. The action certainly did succeed in delaying majority rule, but it also provoked an angry international reaction and rendered inevitable a decade or more of bitter civil war that would soon follow.

Whites in Rhodesia were hopelessly outnumbered by blacks and could not realistically anticipate surviving a conventional war against two guerrilla armies enjoying full Eastern bloc support. The Rhodesian military establishment, despite being heavily supported by regular black army and police personnel, was nonetheless dominated by whites with its survival dependent

Above: The Malayan Scouts, later C Squadron SAS, in the jungle on a rafting patrol. Note the 68lb troop radio on the soldier's back.

Left: Ron Reid-Daly after his first six-week operation during the Malayan Campaign. It was here that he first gained his knowledge of pseudo/counter-insurgency operations.

Rhodesian SAS soldier, Lieutenant A.D.C Webb, after a parachute jump during the Malayan Campaign.

largely on a regular white service core supported by general white conscription and comprehensive territorial obligations. A key survival tactic was the evolution of a culture of innovation and experimentation within the military, supported by an aggressive attack mentality, which succeeded for more than a decade in keeping the large guerrilla armies in Mozambique and Zambia at a constant tactical disadvantage.

To achieve this, the Rhodesian security forces relied heavily on a collection of unique and rather unconventional special force units. The army, for example, made practical use of mounted infantry, versatile platoon-sized police reserve tracker units, conventional special forces in the form of the Special Air Service (SAS), the compact and deadly Rhodesia Light Infantry, and of course the enduringly iconic Selous Scouts.

It all began in the early 1960s with the rise of black political activity in the colony and the inevitable black-on-black factional violence that this catalyzed. The early civil response to this was directed primarily toward keeping the warring factions apart, making exclusive use of police resources with military support available but not directly called upon. It was only after the main political parties had been banned and their leadership imprisoned or restricted that a more organized insurgency emerged that began to direct coordinated attacks against the government and white economic interests. These early incursions tended to be ill conceived and disorganized and were dealt with relatively easily by a combination of police and military resources.

Such was the state of play in the 1960s. By the beginning of the 1970s, however, the situation had deteriorated significantly with the advent of fully fledged armed incursions beginning to take place from bases in Zambia and the Tete Province of Mozambique. However, once again, these were confined to the north and northeast and lacked professionalism. As a consequence they were relatively easily contained.

The watershed year for Rhodesia was 1972. This marked a point at which an amateurish and rather experimental insurgency began its evolution into a mature and fully constituted civil war. By the end of the 1960s the liberation movements—ZAPU the senior and ZANU the junior—had begun to recognize the hopelessness of ill-equipped and ill-trained cadres attempting to match wits and fire with the highly accomplished and well-supported Rhodesian army. A strategy was born that echoed tried and tested revolutionary principles drawn from Mao tse Tung's *Red Book*. Part of this revision of strategy involved recognizing the strengths of the liberation movement and identifying the weaknesses of the Rhodesian army.

The principal weakness of the Rhodesian army and security system in general was its limited size. By 1965 the white population of the colony amounted to no more than 250,000 which at the time was less than the black population of a large urban township. Bearing in mind the size of the country, and despite a continuing reliance on the black rank and file, there were simply too few whites to be in all places at once. The revised guerrilla strategy sought to exploit this signature weakness.

As the 1960s drew to a close and the armed insurgency appeared to subside, an aura of apparent peace settled on the land. The Rhodesian security and intelligence services relaxed somewhat, allowing themselves to be lulled by the notion that the nationalists had been defeated. However, under the surface, ZANU political commissars had been very busy moving among the population of the northeast in an effort to inform the masses of the coming revolution. This process typically involved an intoxicating mix of Marxist orientation and extreme violence. The lesson deployed was simple: *behold the rewards of liberation versus the price of collaboration.* To illustrate the latter point political meetings very often ended with the salutary torture and killing of named 'sell-outs' and political quislings.

Once inside the country and insinuated within compliant local communities the armies of liberation were then able to concentrate on soft and strategic targets which, it was intended, would force the too-small Rhodesian army to over-extend itself. This would, in combination with sanctions, a steady emigration of whites from the country and a constantly expanding battle front, precipitate an inevitable political and economic collapse.

The preparation for this new phase of the war went on right under the noses of the Rhodesian security services. It was only as attacks began to take place in the northeast of Rhodesia with no obvious trace of the insurgents anywhere to be found that the full implication of what was taking place began to be appreciated. Prior to this point, the army had largely employed the simple tactic of cross-grain patrolling in operational areas, followed by tracker-assisted follow-up and contact.

Now incoming insurgents were able to simply merge with a receptive local population in the Tribal Trust Lands, the so-called native reserves, and remain effectively invisible. Intelligence sources dried up. Local people knew nothing and said nothing.

Burning a communist guerrilla camp deep in the Belum Valley jungle on the Siamese border of Malaya. The atap bashas are strikingly similar to those used by ZANLA guerrillas.

Reid-Daly (at left) during a training jump at the RAF Parachute School, Singapore, Malaya.

Bearded and with bush hat turned up, Sergeant Reid-Daly is in a jovial mood, having just returned from a three-month operation in the Malayan jungle.

No rough treatment at the hands of a white security force member had a hope of competing in severity to what the 'terrs' or 'gooks' dished up on an almost nightly basis. The local population was siding with the revolution, hearts and minds were being lost and a drastic review of military strategy was urgently required.

SAS radio operator, Sergeant Billy Conn, in a Malayan paddy field. He is reporting to the aircraft that all is well on the DZ after an operational parachute deployment.

One of the original 'pioneers', Basil Moss, as a flight lieutenant.

Captain Reid-Daly on secondment to the Portuguese army, on operations in Mozambique, 1967.

Winston Hart, Basil Moss and Pat Miller at the temporary Selous Scout camp, Bindura 1974.

The solution was partly home-grown and partly borrowed. The borrowed element can be traced to British counter-insurgency operations in Malaya during the uprising in that colony that began after the Second World War. The innovative tactics developed by the British during this period can be best defined by the architect of the original Malayan 'Hearts and Minds' strategy, General Gerald Templer. It was he who said of counter-insurgency: "The answer lies not in pouring more troops into the jungle, but rests in the hearts and minds of the people. Winning 'hearts and minds' requires understanding the local culture."[1]

In the context of any conflict that could be regarded as a war of independence, or a colonial war, gaining the upper hand in the matter of hearts and minds is extremely difficult because of the obvious cultural conflict that would be associated with an indigenous people ostensibly at war with an occupying power. In the case of Kenya, where pseudo operations were used to great effect against terror gangs affiliated with the Mau Mau, there was rarely any common ground to be found between black and white, and certainly those blacks eager to see the perpetuation of white rule in the country were very few indeed. Here the 'turned guerrilla' concept formed the backbone of counter-terrorism. Blacks, however, were very active on the side of the colonial government in the suppression of the Mau Mau, and many of these were ex-gang members or turned guerrillas.

Key to the evolution of pseudo operations was the development of techniques to quickly turn captured guerrillas to the government side. The psychology of this was very haphazard and evolved less as a science than an art. Kenyan Special Branch agents involved in this work were in fact quite often surprised at the ease with which even high-ranking captures could be turned.

British writer F.D. Corfield, who wrote the definitive historical survey of the Mau Mau, *The Origins and Growth of the Mau Mau*, made an interesting point when considering the psychology of the Kikuyu tribe from which the Mau Mau had emerged. In January 1953 British headlines were dominated by the brutal murder of Kenya farmer Roger Ruck and his family. Ruck had been drawn from his house by a trusted groom who indicated that a terrorist had been captured. Once out in the open Ruck was set upon and brutally beaten and hacked to death. His wife ran outside to help and was similarly dealt with. The gang then entered the house to search for the couple's six-year-old son, Michael, who was located cowering in terror in his bedroom where he was also hacked to death.

What was inexplicable to whites both in Kenya and the UK were the actions of the Kikuyu groom, a man who had been commended just a few days earlier for tenderly carrying home an injured Michael Ruck after the child had been violently thrown from his horse.

WOII Al Tourle, RLI, poses next to some dead guerrillas he has just shot. During the 1960s, the Rhodesian army enjoyed considerable success against the enemy in the largely uninhabited Zambezi Valley. Without the succour of a civilian population to assist the guerrillas, it was simply a question of following up spoor and killing them.

A civilian bus in the rural area, shortly after detonating a landmine. The landmine was a terror weapon of choice for the guerrillas.
Photo: Neville Spurr

This perceived duality of nature of the Kikuyu would become a common and accepted feature of the white view of Mau Mau, and later of the white Rhodesian view of its own nationalist guerrillas. Corfield then went on to remark on the effect this duality would have on the Mau Mau itself:

> On surrender, a gangster, who had been in the forest for years, and had taken a succession of the vilest of Mau Mau oaths, almost immediately volunteered to lead security forces to the hideout of his previous gang and, if an opportunity arose, would willingly dispose of his recent comrades in arms.[2]

Another common feature of pseudo operations within the British stable has been the fact that development has been driven by police under Special Branch and not military intelligence as might be expected. Special Branch within the British and Commonwealth model has tended to be that arm of the security services concerned primarily with national security. Military intelligence by its nature is concerned with military affairs and cannot be expected to be attuned to developments within the wider population of a society within which an insurgency is underway. Information gathered to assist and develop pseudo operations naturally emerges from within the civilian population, and Special Branch, as an arm of the police, is ideally positioned to exploit it.

In the case of Kenya there was considerable cooperation between the army and Special Branch. Military personnel were seconded from the Kenya Regiment to serve as Field Intelligence Assistants, or FIAs, posted to outlying areas of the district and tasked to help gather information. Once this system had been established, army headquarters began assigning army officers at district level as District Military Intelligence Officers to work in conjunction with Special Branch. It was not until much later that an army officer was assigned to Special Branch headquarters to serve as the principal liaison to coordinate the operations of the army and Special Branch nationally.

In the case of Southern Rhodesia, Special Branch grew out of the perceived need for an internal intelligence organ to keep abreast of urban industrial unrest that took place in the late 1940s and 1950s. Prior to this, and thanks to the fact that the BSAP had traditionally been, and largely remained, the main functioning military force in the country, all operational intelligence gathering had been undertaken from resources within the force itself. Special Branch was formed from, and remained a section of, the BSAP Criminal Investigation Department, or CID. Systems and training closely followed the British pattern of MI5 with a number of the early members of Special Branch receiving specialist training from MI5. British liaison representatives, and indeed members of the American CIA, both originating from their respective embassies, were represented at Special Branch headquarters under the expected rules of cooperation at that time. These men helped a great deal with early training.

Special Branch was very active during the township unrest of the 1960s, gathering information to assist the police effort. From here the first evidence emerged of individuals leaving the country for military training abroad. At that time Rhodesian CID handled the Bechuanaland (which became independent Botswana in 1966) Police fingerprinting work which was necessary to keep abreast of floods of migrant labour moving through the region. This was easily adapted by the Rhodesians to maintain records of individuals among these leaving Rhodesia via Botswana for training in China or the Soviet Union. From that point it was also relatively easy to plant black operatives among those entering training who were able to provide detailed and accurate intelligence.

From this it was a fairly natural progression for Special Branch to become increasingly involved in the gathering of intelligence to assist in military operations as well as for the purpose of gaining a general picture of the state of the insurgency in the northeast. Military intelligence in Rhodesia had traditionally been weak—marking waterholes on maps, as Special Branch tended to see it. Units below brigade level usually had only a corporal for their intelligence officer.

Early days: an RLI stick on operations in the Zambezi Valley in the 1960s.

Early landmine incident. *Photo: Neville Spurr*

The job of intelligence officers at all levels was, according to Rhodesian counter-insurgency expert Jackie Cilliers, "to be filled by someone not suitable for any other post. It was also considered the first ready-use pool of officers and other ranks, should a shortage of personnel occur elsewhere".[3]

As a consequence, the use of pseudo operations in Rhodesia was as much an innovation of the civilian intelligence community as it had been in Kenya and Malaya. History has tended to portray the Director-General of the Central Intelligence Organization, the inscrutable and enigmatic Ken Flower, as the midwife of the concept, but in practical terms it began as a Special Branch operation and in many respects that is how it remained.

It is also true that no single organization or person can realistically lay claim to the original idea of the Selous Scouts, since in reality it evolved somewhat as a natural extension of work already underway in a number of intelligence quarters. However, those that do claim to have been responsible for the early development of pseudo tactics in Rhodesia forswear any suggestion that inspiration might have been drawn either from Kenya or Malaya, although of course, it is difficult to state categorically that the one was not an extension of the other. Similar responses to similar situations would naturally evolve, but it is unlikely that those pondering groundbreaking ideas to cope with a rapidly manifesting situation would not seek ideas from outside their own narrow pool of talent. It is worth mentioning that Ian Henderson, one of those credited with developing the concept in Rhodesia, was briefly involved with Special Branch in Rhodesia and would hardly have been mute on the matter.

In fact Rhodesian observers needed only to look across the border to Mozambique for practical inspiration. The Portuguese in both Mozambique and Angola made use of pseudo units in dealing with their own black nationalist insurgencies. Known as *Flechas*, or Arrows, these were usually highly proficient, platoon-sized units consisting of local tribesmen and turned rebels operating on a simple bounty system. The unit was formed by Dr Sáo José Lopes, at the time head of the Portuguese intelligence service, the *Direcção Geral de Segurança*. Flecha groups were notable for their use of Bushmen operatives, usually recruited from the Kazamba Tribe, and known locally as *Zama*, or *Kwengo*. Flecha units enjoyed considerable success during Portugal's African wars, accounting at one stage for some 60 per cent of guerrillas killed on operations.[4]

It could also be said that the embryo of the highly organized system of pseudo operations later developed by the Selous Scouts was fertilized by the simple ruse of a plain-clothed policeman attempting to appear less conspicuous by abandoning his uniform. One of these was Special Branch Detective Section Officer Winston Hart who, from his office in Bindura, spent long periods of time in Mozambique immersed in the Portuguese war effort and prolifically gathering information to add to the already comprehensive Special Branch intelligence picture. Hart liaised with seven separate police stations in the northeast of Rhodesia, with plain-clothed, ground-coverage units in each one

Neville Spurr, a Special Branch operative, grins with relief, having escaped injury from a landmine detonation. SB operatives in the rural areas faced a dangerous and lonely existence. *Photo: Neville Spurr*

Wafa Wafa training camp accommodation. From left: Scotty Drysdale, Andy Kockett, Colin Blythewood and Nigel Hughes.

of these who were responsible for gathering information in their immediate locality.

It would be natural that around this sort of highly specialized work innovation would germinate, and in fact Hart managed his own informal pseudo team made up of black BSAP personnel who worked among the local rural population gathering intelligence. The matter had also been frequently raised by army lieutenant Allan Savory, a renowned Rhodesian ecologist, tracker and political theorist, in his work with the Rhodesian SAS which was itself increasingly engaged in covert activities in Mozambique.

Savory, although never a member of the Selous Scouts, was nonetheless something of a founder member with regards to his ongoing promotion of the *style* of soldiering that would evolve, in a few short years, into the Selous Scouts. Savory argued frequently that in order to effectively fight the kind of war that was emerging, it would be necessary to place a higher dependence on trained specialists fluent in precisely the operational environment wherein the insurgency was taking place, and no less imbibed with the cultural peculiarities of the local blacks that made up the enemy.

This obviously would require the formation and deployment of small teams, lightly armed and equipped, that could move quietly and effectively in the actual environment of war and with command devolved down to the stick or squad level. The obvious initial source of manpower for this type of unit would be the farming, professional hunting and wildlife-management community which in Rhodesia made up a small but committed clique of white African 'bushmen'. From this the Tracker Combat Unit (TCU) was formed. The unit was manned primarily by territorials and administered by the School of Infantry in Gwelo. The School of Infantry, incidentally, also administered the Army Tracking Wing which was based at Kariba and configured to train and develop trackers for the regular army.

In the meanwhile, the first attempts to form and deploy Flecha-style psuedo units took place in operations against ZANLA (Zimbabwe African National Liberation Army) and Frelimo (*Frente de Libertação de Moçambique*) in Mozambique during the late 1960s. These were authorized by Ken Flower, who commented

rather cryptically on the matter in his 1987 memoir, *Serving Secretly*:

As the pressures of war developed, we found ourselves having to play in the more open field of counter-action against the countries concerned, starting with Zambia. We kept our counter-action in low key for as long as possible, providing disinformation (or 'grey propaganda') which led, for example, to ZIPRA (Zimbabwe People's Revolutionary Army) taking most of the blame for the deaths of Zambian civilians or for accidents involving their colleagues in ZANU. It also became necessary to bring some of our agents in the nationalist movements under the operational control of Special Branch, or under men in the services with specialist knowledge. This led to the formation in 1966 of the first 'pseudo terrorist' groups, which included turned guerrillas as they became available. From these groups evolved the Selous Scouts at a later date.[5]

This characteristically oblique series of references pertain to the 'special operations' which covered many of the covert activities taking place under the remit of the CIO, from high-profile political assassinations to the development of the MNR (*Resistência Nacional Moçambicana*), or Renamo, an ersatz rebellion created by the CIO in order to destabilize a newly independent Mozambique, and supported and trained largely by C Squadron SAS.

From here the baton was passed to Special Branch via its Officer Commanding, Senior Assistant Commissioner Bill Crabtree, who was responsible for the first official training course to be offered in pseudo tactics. This course was designed and conducted in the remote southeast of Rhodesia, adjacent to the Gona re Zhou National Park, by Lieutenant Allan Savory who instructed 12 men drawn from the SAS, Special Branch and the CID in the fundamentals of tracking, bush-craft and survival.

Tracking and bush-craft were obviously pivotal skills in the successful development of a pseudo operator for African conditions but, perhaps more important still, as Templer himself

The first Selous Scout instructional team at the Army Tracking Wing, Kariba, 1975. From left: Noel Robey, Bruce Bartlett, John Ashburner, Pete Clemence, Anthony White and Martinus 'Bushpig' Kok.

Jeremy Strong, the first 2IC of the Selous Scouts, seen here as an RLI major, being awarded the Member of the Legion of Merit (Combatant) by President John Wrathall

had noted, would have been an idiomatic command of one or other of the main local native languages and a working familiarity with the nuances of black lifestyle, mannerisms and culture. Such white men did exist within the rural heartland of Rhodesia, and in mining and industry where blacks and whites worked in close commerce, but on the whole these men were rare.

This did not present any particular problem in the short term, as initial experiments and early operational trials tended to be very limited and quite experimental. There was also, at that time, less interest shown in gaining actual operational kills than in gathering intelligence on guerrilla incursions that were still widely dispersed, erratic and not overtly threatening.

To appreciate the contemporary security situation in Rhodesia one need only bear in mind that both liberation movements were based primarily in Zambia from where they mounted armed incursions. This meant that available access routes into Rhodesia were limited to the northern border region and held in check in the east by the fact that Portugal still enjoyed more or less definitive territorial control over Mozambique. This gave the Rhodesian security forces an almost unassailable defensive advantage inasmuch as no entry into Rhodesia was possible other than to cross the Zambezi River into the waiting arms of Rhodesian troops. Any that succeeded in penetrating this security cordon would find the blistering and waterless expanse of the Zambezi Valley lying between them and the sanctuary of the populated heartland.

Matters changed with both the revised guerrilla policy of the early 1970s and with early signs of slippage of the Portuguese security presence in the north of Mozambique. Operation *Hurricane* was launched as a response to this, which in due course became the first ongoing operation, and the first of a number of permanent Joint Operational Centres (JOCs) that would in due course divide the country into seven operational sectors. This in itself marked a clear end to what had been known as the phoney war, or the non-war of the 1960s. Concern at the higher levels of command suddenly became acute and the need for intelligence urgent. Here at last were the ideal conditions for the development of an organized and supported programme of pseudo operations.

The commander of Operation *Hurricane* at that time was Brigadier John Hickman, a precocious and somewhat independent-minded man who often found himself at odds with the stifling orthodoxy of the Rhodesian high command. He happened also to be one of those few commanders in the army who were interested in pseudo reconnaissance, which was fortunate, for without his support and assistance—or perhaps more accurately, had he chosen to actively oppose it, as many did—the men of Special Branch would have had a far more difficult time in launching the project than they ultimately did.

Meetings were held every evening at the Centenary JOC which included members of the army and Special Branch. On one particular evening the discussion centred around plans to deal with a local medium carrying the pseudonym Nehanda who was active in the liberation movement in Mozambique. The use of a pseudo team was proposed and agreed upon. It was suggested by the army that white volunteers be sought from the tracking unit to be backed up by a handful of soldiers from the RAR and informed by recent guerrilla captures supplied by Special Branch.

An early lesson that had been learned by the use of black pseudo teams was, for whatever reason this might have been, that blacks lacked the aggressive fighting spirit in an open fight. Initially this hardly mattered since it was intelligence and not kills being sought, and so long as their fundamental loyalty remained intact, how they fought did not matter. If a dramatic result was sought, however, it was concluded that white team leaders would be

Stretch Franklin (clothed) marshals recruits for the evening swim at Wafa Wafa training camp, Kariba, during selection course.

essential. Hence the call for white volunteers. This, as has been noted, would be exacting work requiring a high level of tactical proficiency in combination with good language and cultural fluency. Individuals meeting these requirements were not easy to find. Sergeants André Rabie and Stretch Franklin, however, were two such men. Both were members of the SAS, both spoke the required native languages—Franklin indifferently but Rabie far more fluently—and both were keenly interested in the scheme. The two had been conducting their own informal experiments for some time but joined forces with Special Branch, at which point they began to train and function in a more coordinated way. Special Branch Detective Section Officer Peter Stanton ran a course which was, in effect, a comprehensive intelligence brief of what was known to date of the ZANLA structure, its system of local cell organization, its chain of command and the specific protocols and terminologies that were used in recognition and authentication.

Here lay arguably the main point of stress of the pseudo theory such as it stood. Even though ZANLA was not generally aware of what was afoot, it operated using a system of code words and other security tripwires that enabled insurgent groups to recognize one another and to interact in the field. In order to succeed this sort of information needed to be updated moment upon moment, and would require freshly captured and turned insurgents in order to keep the pseudo groups in the field informed and current.

A fact that worked very much to the advantage of Special Branch was that ZANLA units in the field were not supplied with radio communications. This required them to use a convoluted system of communication between active groups, their rear bases and the central command structure. Because up-to-the-minute changes could not be rapidly communicated, strategies and systems were rigidly dependent on the written-message system. This removed any local discretion or capacity for rapid reaction, but more importantly it had the effect of forcing the guerrilla units to

commit every detail of their activity and objectives to paper. This in turn tended to regularly reward Special Branch with massive intelligence bonanzas.

Thus, armed with all this new intelligence information, and with the practical addition of two very recently turned captures, the pseudo teams were deployed once again and, once again, it was found that huge potential was evident, but that something fundamental was missing. The project lacked an *identity*. It was neither Special Branch nor army, yet a little bit of both. The entire business was in fact viewed by the officers running Operation *Hurricane* as little more than an encumbrance. The pseudos needed to be housed, requisitioned and fed which presented peculiar difficulties, bearing in mind that secrecy was the key and that a handful of those operating were ex-guerrillas who could hardly be housed among regular troops. The police and Internal Affairs were irritated because their safe houses were being overrun by the army without any plausible explanation which all tended to point to the fact that something needed to be done.

Special Branch Detective Section Officer Winston Hart brought the matter to the attention of his commanding officer, Peter Tomlinson, and for his trouble was rewarded with the task of formally coordinating the entire operation. This now gave it a certain amount of legitimacy with which it could begin to establish itself upon its own resources. An important addition to the emerging unit was Flight Lieutenant Basil Moss of the Rhodesian Air Force (RhAF) who brought with him a recognized linguistic skill. It was said of Moss that he could converse with a blindfolded capture, offering no hint whatsoever that it was a white man talking. This was something very unique indeed. Moss, however, was older, in his early 40s at the time, although this did not in any way appear to inhibit his operational capacity which continued for some time to come. Robin Hughes joined from National Parks, which was a natural source of the kind of men who would unsurprisingly be drawn to this sort of work.

The horizontal rope on the selection assault course at Wafa Wafa. The 34-foot drop is into thorn bush.

Tigns Oelof and Andy Kockett pose with their home-made bush webbing, during selection course.

Success under these new arrangements was immediate in terms of a rapid inflow of good intelligence. The initial focus was not on attempting to fool genuine guerrilla groups but to fool the local people into informing on the movements and whereabouts of genuine groups.

The early belief that a white operator could disguise himself as a black man and effectively pose as a guerrilla was in fact proved to be impossible 90 per cent of the time. White team leaders therefore led very much from the rear. It was agreed that one white operator on deployment with a team of blacks, some of whom would be recent captures, would be impractical and dangerous. Hart instituted a policy of deploying two white operatives per team,

André Rabie.
Source: Jonathan Pittaway

which at that point meant effectively Franklin and Rabie.

A quick glance at a topographical map of the Operation *Hurricane* area is enough to get a sense of the broad geographical layout of the region. The landscape is dominated by the Zambezi Valley, across which any insurgent group would be required to traverse in order to get into Rhodesia. Having achieved this, it would thereafter be a fairly simple matter of mounting the Zambezi escarpment and accessing the cool uplands and the populated Tribal Trust Lands beyond. The escarpment is cut by a good many smaller rivers that feed into the Zambezi itself, which at that time provided a system of natural highways inland for incoming guerrilla groups. Once above the valley, these rivers tended to host large rural populations wherein sanctuary was available to insurgent groups for recuperation and safe bases from which to launch operations.

In August 1973 it was proposed that Rabie, Franklin and their pseudo team be dropped by helicopter in Mozambique and follow one of these natural inland routes, the Ruya River, posing as an incoming ZANLA unit. The operation was codenamed *The Long Walk*. Hart, flown into the region by helicopter every few days, met with and debriefed both men, briefing them in turn as new trends and information relevant to their operation surfaced.

One day Hart received a call from the team with the news that they had a capture. He was flown in just before dark and was met by the team who walked him into the hills. The information was that they had captured a young armed *mujiba*. (*Mujibas* were not fully fledged guerrillas but somewhat more than local contact men; they were normally youths, sometimes armed, who made up the grassroots ZANU network.) The information volunteered indicated that a large meeting was about to take place, including a significant group that was shortly due in the country.

Hart intended to return to Mount Darwin with the capture but paused at Rabie's suggestion that they be allowed keep him and use him to lead them to the meeting. This was reluctantly agreed to, after which the man was brought over from a separate camp and introduced to Hart. At that point he was presented with two clear options: he could either be handed over to the official agents of law and order, after which he could commence his journey to the gallows via the due process of law, or he could agree to work with the group, in which case he would enjoy official protection. Under the circumstances this decision was easily and quickly made. The man was handed back his firearm—minus its firing pin—and returned to the field in the company of the Rhodesian army.

Rabie was pulled off the operation shortly after to lend his tracking skills to the follow-up of a landmine incident elsewhere in the district, leaving Franklin alone. In due course the promised meeting was held. A tight and ferocious contact followed that resulted in the death of a senior ZANLA guerrilla leader, but not the bulk of the group who all managed to escape. The next day an RLI follow-up revealed a second fatality some 100 metres from the scene of the contact, and blood spoor indicating two walking wounded. A third fatality was located some months later.

When he heard the news Rabie could hardly wait to get back in and claim his hackles. Franklin, meanwhile, was pulled out in the aftermath of the contact for a brief R&R. Shortly after, a snippet of intelligence found its way through the orthodox channels, indicating the presence of guerrillas in the area. A careful crosscheck of Rabie's position ruled out his group as a possible source of the tip, after which the RLI moved in to intercept the group and take them out.

Rabie, however, had misread his position and provided a faulty map reference. He was ten kilometres north of his stated position and was surprised by the RLI hunter/killer team. A brief concentration of fire followed and Rabie was shot dead.

A second tragedy occurred just a month later with the death in action of territorial officer Lieutenant Robin Hughes. Despite this shocking series of reverses it was clear that the pseudo concept was suddenly beginning to gain traction. Several successful actions followed the *The Long Walk*, each of which turned up a respectable tally of kills. As a corollary to this, successful captures also increased, most of which were turned, adding to the general efficiency of operations, which in turn helped raise its profile and ensure its continued existence.

Word of all this soon reached the desk of CIO Director-General Ken Flower. The initial concept had been his and he was pleased that, after several false starts, it was at last beginning to prove its worth. The moment now seemed favourable to take the next step toward proper organization. A suggestion to this effect was made to Lieutenant-General Peter Walls— commander of the army at that time—who consulted Prime Minister Ian Smith. Smith in turn gave his enthusiastic approval. This was sufficient to overcome an institutionalized reluctance within the military itself and moves toward the establishment of a dedicated pseudo regiment commenced.

The process of moulding the experimental pseudo teams into an organized unit began with the choice of commanding officer. The job was given to Captain Ron Reid-Daly, retired, recently of the RLI. Much has been said in the years about the choice of Reid-Daly for this job. On the surface he was not ideally qualified. He had not been commissioned through selection and training in a military academy such as Sandhurst, as many Rhodesian officers had, nor locally through the School of Infantry. He had worked his way up through the ranks and been commissioned during his later service with the RLI. In military circles this led to a certain amount of comment, and certainly in years to come his rapid promotion and command of one of Rhodesia's most celebrated special force units engendered much professional jealously and

inter-unit rivalry. Perhaps the best explanation for his appointment is that Reid-Daly happened to be available. His retirement from the army was premised on his own belief that he had reached the limit of his professional progress and wished to seek new pastures. Winston Hart was among a number of serving members of the security services who recognized that the army was about to lose a good man. He and the future commander of the Special Branch Selous Scouts liaison, Mac McGuinness, discussed the possibility of bringing Reid-Daly into Special Branch. However, the announcement of his resignation coincided perfectly with the authorization of plans to form the regiment.

As a military man Reid-Daly enjoyed certain advantages. The fact that he did not belong to the elite of commissioned officers— who themselves never belonged to the soldiering class—gave him a degree of access to the rank and file that was unique. His man-management skills were exemplary. He was feared by his men despite having a reputation for unusual compassion, but was universally loved and admired by those who served under him—men who to this day protect the legacy of their founding commander with an almost fanatical loyalty. Perhaps his greatest advantage was that he and General Walls knew one another and were on friendly terms.

Reid-Daly also had a maverick streak that was perhaps not immediately obvious within the orthodox institution of the RLI, but which found a home within the unorthodox structure and operational techniques that would evolve under his command of the Selous Scouts. In this regard he found a natural place among many other no less individualistic special force commanders within the British military family. First among equals here was without doubt the mercurial and brilliant T.E. Lawrence, of Lawrence of Arabia fame. Lawrence spoke Arabic fluently and displayed a sometimes venal fondness for ethnic dress. This might have played to his vanity a little, but it worked almost perfectly as a disguise among the Arab tribes—*almost* because Lawrence could do nothing about his blue eyes, and he suffered accordingly.

Others include Brigadier-General Clement Leslie Smith of the Imperial Camel Corps, Major-General Arthur Reginald Chater of the Somaliland Camel Corps, Orde Wingate, founder of the Gideon Force and the Chindits, and Wilfred Thesiger, who served in the Gideon Force as well as the SAS and the Long Range Desert Group, the creations of David Stirling and Sir Ralph Bagnold respectively. All these men shared one common trait: they were capable of lateral thought and as a consequence struggled within a military bureaucracy traditionally sternly resistant to innovation and individuality.

Reid-Daly would experience all this and more. He was a man of both great fortune and misfortune. When offered the command of a new unit of such unusual configuration he was being offered a unique place in military history, but at the same time he was being handed a poison chalice that would counter-balance every achievement with equal disapprobation and difficulty within the very institutions that he served. There are few who have studied the existence of the Selous Scouts who would not apportion at

Selection course, Wafa Wafa. Back blisters at the end of the 90-kilometre endurance march. The soldiers had to carry a 35kg pack filled with rocks plus webbing, rifle and ammunition.

Selection course, Wafa Wafa. Butchering a rotting elephant carcass for rations.

Relief shows on the faces of these soldiers at the end of their selection course. At their feet is the hated log that they have had to lug around for days.

least some blame for his difficulties upon himself, but Reid-Daly could at least say this in honest reflection: albeit late in his career, the defining mandate that revealed him as a brilliant military commander, for better or worse, was given to him. There are many other, more brilliant men perhaps than he, for whom that opportunity simply never arises.

According to Reid-Daly himself, there was a considerable amount of discourse between him and army commander Peter Walls before the appointment was finalized. He had, under pressure from his wife, already decided on his retirement from the army. However, for a career soldier, the offer of a return to uniform with the rank of major and to take on what would, without doubt, be a superbly adventurous task was simply too tempting. To his wife's chagrin he accepted, and thus a legend within a legend was born.

What Reid-Daly had to offer was long military experience with the requisite balance of staff and operational service. He had in fact begun his career as a volunteer in the Rhodesian contingent earmarked to serve in Korea. This group, later diverted to Malaya, was the formative Rhodesian C Squadron SAS, the Malayan Scouts, and it was here that Reid-Daly gained his first rite of fire. After three years' service in that theatre, service that covered the spectrum of deep-penetration operations, he returned to Rhodesia

and joined the regular army. In 1961 he became the formative Regimental Sergeant-Major for the RLI, being commissioned in 1964 and retired, ostensibly, in 1974.

Before assuming his new command Reid-Daly left the country for a holiday in the Greek islands with a great deal of food for thought. In his absence the technocrats of the Prime Minister's Office and the CIO laboured over the technicalities of the new unit, and in particular its terms of reference. The directive when it was complete read as follows:

> The unit came into being following a directive issued by the Prime Minister to the Director-General of the CIO who was in turn promised the full cooperation of the Commissioner of Police and the Army Commander to staff and equip the same. It was tasked to carry out operations of a clandestine nature wherever it may be called upon to serve, drawing its manpower from the combined services and other less obvious channels [turned guerrillas], while receiving instruction from the OCC, Director-General CIO, Service Commanders and operational JOCs.[6]

The directive went on to define the chain of command and

Tracking course. Pete Clemence and Sergeant Dzingai 'on spoor'.

Fresh rations during selection course.

organizational structure of the proposed unit. Ken Flower would remain overall commander of pseudo operations, undertaking to appraise the Commissioner of Police on all operations, while Walls would assume responsibility for military logistics and personnel. Mention was made of the role of the proposed unit in the clandestine elimination of guerrillas *both within and without the country*. Special Branch liaison officers were accounted for, most notably Winston Hart, who were to be commanded by Superintendent Mac McGuinness.

The Selous Scout Regiment—the name was derived from an earlier armoured car unit of the same name that had disbanded, making the name available among a number of other possible choices—would thereafter exist as two distinct branches. The military and regimental command of the unit would reside with Reid-Daly, but the intelligence complement, a large and important aspect of the Selous Scouts existence, would fall under the remit of Mac McGuinness.

It is interesting to note here that this deployment of Special Branch liaison personnel to the new 'tracking' unit would sow the seeds of a clear division of loyalty within this organization. Special Branch and Special Branch Selous Scouts would devolve eventually into two distinctly separate and, for the most part, mutually antagonistic offices.

The end of the phoney war set in motion the rapid militarization of Rhodesian society. As a consequence, manpower was universally in both short supply and high demand. This complicated matters for Reid-Daly as he set about selecting the formative personnel for administration and training. A large part of the problem lay in the fact that the Selous Scout Regiment was hiding behind the pretence that its sole function was tracking, which made absolutely no sense to irritated staff officers responsible for supplying inflated kit requirements solely on the say-so of an over-promoted sergeant-major like Reid-Daly. In his memoir Reid-Daly records many bruising clashes with senior staff officers, most of which were ultimately resolved only by direct appeal to General Walls who usually came down on the side of his proxy. All this was quite understandable, bearing in mind the secret nature of the Selous

Scouts, and what was planned for it, but it created a great deal of early friction that would grow in due course to impact the Selous Scouts very deeply.

Reid-Daly's singular advantage in fulfilling a difficult mission was this direct and open line of communication with Peter Walls. To his credit he made use of it sparingly but it was not unheard of for him to knock on the general's door when all else failed. The net result was that Reid-Daly ended up having to balance out his one heavyweight friend with a great many lightweight enemies. Notwithstanding the increasing interest being shown by the NCOs and junior officers of the security forces in what was afoot in the Selous Scouts, at a command level Reid-Daly won very few admirers, and the Selous Scouts itself very few friends.

However, there was a job to be done and Reid-Daly did it. He wrestled with problems of staffing, recruitment, equipment and housing, locating after a great deal of trouble a home base in an old Empire Air Training facility situated just off the main Salisbury–Kariba road and some 25 miles northwest of the capital. Inkomo had originally been a bombing range so it was spread over a significant area—some 13,000 acres all told—which gave it the privacy and isolation that was necessary, while also positioning the unit's headquarters more or less equidistant from all of the border regions, anticipating, as was becoming more likely every day, a rapid expansion of the war. The original Selous Scout home in an isolated corner of Trojan nickel mine near Bindura remained the home of the Special Branch Selous Scouts.

Inkomo Barracks became something of an institution. As the Selous Scouts expanded the barracks, the surrounds developed almost into a township with the relocation into its protected environment of the families of turned guerrillas who would most certainly have suffered retribution from the guerrillas once word became general that they had defected. This included a school and a church among many other facilities.

Reid-Daly was assisted, incidentally, by his 2IC, Captain, later Major, Jeremy Strong. Strong was in many ways the polar opposite of Reid-Daly. He was a Sandhurst-trained officer with significant combat experience and a recipient of the Bronze Cross

Above left: Stretch Franklin. *Source: Jonathan Pittaway*; centre: Franklin 'takes five' in the bush. He and André Rabie were founding members of the Selous Scouts.

Recruits eating raw liver during survival course.

of Rhodesia. He was at that time serving as an instructor at the School of Infantry in Gwelo. Strong provided some orthodox ballast and conventional soldierly organization to the unit. It is interesting to note in this regard that he was never in line to take over the regiment should Reid-Daly leave or retire. For his own part Strong had no interest in this possibility. In a conversation between him and Winston Hart, Strong confided that he felt misplaced in an environment that required unconventional and lateral thought, as opposed to Reid-Daly who, for better or worse, was perfectly willing to think out of the box. In Strong's opinion the Selous Scouts was not a military unit but a Special Branch unit. It was his intention to remain only as long as it would take him to assist in getting the unit off the ground, although, in the event, he remained longer than this before eventually leaving to return to his original home, the RLI.[7]

The next issue to be dealt with was recruitment. Currently the Selous Scouts, such as it was, consisted of Sergeant Stretch Franklin and Captain Basil Moss. To this was added Lieutenant Dale Collett, a South African who had been commissioned in the Rhodesian African Rifles, and Sergeant Charlie Krause of the RLI Tracking Troop who had served under Reid-Daly during his period as officer commanding Support Group RLI. For the remainder Walls gave Reid-Daly a free hand in tapping the regular battalions, in particular the Rhodesian African Rifles, which he did.

His first port of call was the Tracker Combat Unit and the Army Tracking Wing. The TCU, it must be remembered, were territorial soldiers. This was a bold experiment for the times. According to Reid-Daly: "I drafted and signed a circular letter which I ordered to be sent to every man in the Combat Tracker Unit, introducing myself and telling them of the formation of the Selous Scouts. I made the point that, in the new regiment, a territorial soldier would not be regarded as a second-class citizen when compared with a regular soldier. It was the brown beret and

the badge that would count." The entire TCU was called up and evaluated for suitability in the new unit. Out of 65 men only 14 qualified. Reid-Daly later admitted that his decision to introduce territorials into the regiment was less about fostering equality within the ranks than camouflaging his objective. "I must admit," Reid-Daly later wrote, "I was not particularly enthralled of taking territorial soldiers on Selous Scout strength. At that time, with the need for stringent secrecy, I could see little use for them within the main concept envisioned for the regiment. I could, however, see the advantages of using them to create an effective cover to conceal our true role." In due course Reid-Daly would see the matter very differently.

Initial proposals were that the unit should be of company strength, perhaps 120 officers and men. The command element would be all white, with the highest rank to which a black soldier could aspire then being a colour sergeant. Organization would be configured along the same lines as that in the insurgent organizations, which meant, in practice, that each section would consist of eight men. These could be broken down into two tracker-combat teams of four men each, also reflecting the standard tracker configuration which would help maintain cover of the regiment being no more than a specialist tracking unit.

A complete section would comprise a white colour sergeant as the section commander with a half section—or tracker-combat team—consisting in the first part of a sergeant, a lance-corporal and two troopers, and in the second a full corporal, a lance-corporal and two troopers. The troop, consisting of three sections of eight men, or six tracker-combat teams of four men each, would be commanded by a lieutenant, with a warrant officer (second class) as second-in-command. In the initial stages both these posts would be occupied by whites.

In the meanwhile, a disused border-patrol camp situated just outside Makuti on the Zambezi escarpment was identified as a likely training camp. Here the high number of prospective recruits, originating mainly from the SAS and the RLI, would be put through the first selection course. There was a notable absence of black recruits in the first instance which, bearing in mind the preponderance of blacks soldiers in the regular army, was highly suggestive of pressure within the command structure of the Rhodesian African Rifles to keep their best men in the ranks. This was understandable, and it took some shrewd persuasion and another appeal to General Walls for Reid-Daly to shift that particular log jam.

Thus the first volunteers to arrive at Makuti were white. Reid-Daly wanted to brief these men before he dealt with the blacks, presenting to them what he believed would be the defining principle of the Selous Scouts: that the regiment was to be entirely non-racial in character. As Reid-Daly himself put it: "My purpose was not to try and produce European-type soldiers from Africans, but to make very good African soldiers out of them instead."

What Reid-Daly hoped to produce was a functioning amalgam of the best of both black and white military customs. Bearing in mind that the principal *modus operandi* of the unit was to effectively impersonate black, communist-trained guerrillas operating within their own social medium, this was the very least that he needed to achieve. However, he let it be known to the white recruits that black recruits, who would soon follow, would not be told of their intended pseudo role until they had successfully passed selection. Those who did not would pass back into the regular infantry ranks of the army none the wiser.

It ought not to be understated that any racial overlap beyond the strictly formal relationships of the military caste structure was frowned upon both within the military and without. Rhodesia was by no means as racially polarized as was South Africa at that time, but it was a society nonetheless sharply divided along racial lines. The fact that the vast majority of men in the uniformed services were black did not within itself smudge those clear lines. Europeans, i.e. whites, served with Africans only in command roles, and did so within the paternalistic and somewhat patronizing formula of race relations of the period. Thus it must be appreciated that the objective of the Selous Scouts, and indeed what to a very large extent it achieved, was to remove racial barriers from its day-to-day operations. Blacks initially served under the same terms as anywhere else in the Rhodesian army, being limited in promotion prospects of senior NCO rank. However, in due course blacks were commissioned, and many commissioned black Selous Scouts, some of whom were ex-guerrillas, achieved great distinction in the ranks of the regiment.

However, the removal of such entrenched social mores was not easily achieved. The tool that Reid-Daly devised to exorcise the worst racial antipathy from both black and white in the ranks of the Selous Scouts was initially the selection course. Interdependence in the interests of moral survival would also be the key to physical survival on the battlefield. The prototype selection course that was formulated to put this first generation of recruits through their paces was largely the same as that which would remain in place for the remainder of the war. It was informed somewhat

by Reid-Daly's own training within the SAS, but refined and modified by the requirements of the specific role intended for the unit, and the specific environment that it could expect to operate in: the southern Africa bush. This consisted in the main of Highveld-type *miombo* woodland, lowveld *mopane* woodland and the highland forests common to the east of the country.

Reid-Daly also had occasion to study the methods of the Flecha units, and although, like most Rhodesians, he held a poor view of the rank and file of the Portuguese army, he was impressed with both the standards and methods of training being applied to the Flechas and their general *esprit de corps* and combat fitness. In particular, the discipline of silence imposed on individual members throughout the day embedded the routines of non-verbal communication until they became second nature. Meals were taken standing up with great care taken to avoid any kind of noise. Besides this, the unit was subject to continuous repetitions of basic drills in field-craft, weapons training, range work and foot and arms drills on the parade ground. This did not conform entirely to Reid-Daly's sense of what was required of the Selous Scouts but he was nonetheless impressed by the example set by the Portuguese.[1]

The first Selous Scout selection course consisted of the usual shock tactics of hard physical endurance combined with an intense programme of bush-craft and tracking. It is interesting to observe from Reid-Daly's own accounts of the programme, his assessment of black soldiers. He had had little prior exposure to black troops and in his determination to smooth out any suggestion of racial inequality in the ranks of the Selous Scouts, he sought to identify the strengths of those that had volunteered for selection.

Initially he was impressed with the innate bush sensibility and awareness that black soldiers displayed. Most white soldiers were aware of this fact. Those who had scant respect for the aggressive fighting qualities of the black man would rarely be incautious enough to doubt his ability to make optimum use of his natural surroundings. This was evident in an instinctive understanding of both the identification and interpretative aspects of tracking and in unassisted bush navigation at night when using neither a compass nor a map.

Reid-Daly, in common with most Rhodesian whites at that time, subscribed to the commonly held belief that the two tribal divisions in Rhodesia—the Mashona and the amaNdebele—differed from one another primarily in their sense of aggression. Coinciding with the arrival of the white man into the territory, there existed a balance of power between these two groups that steeply favoured the amaNdebele. This group, derived from the

[1] Ken Flower spoke for many Rhodesians, and no doubt quite accurately, when he commented on a meeting with Portuguese military commander, Francisco da Costa Gomes. Gomes leaned over to his military attaché and asked the question: "But do the Rhodesians really expect us to follow their example, living like animals in the African bush merely to confront guerrillas?" "No, *senhor*," the attaché replied, "it is the example that is quite magnificent, and it suits the Rhodesians, who are Anglo-Saxons, but they don't really expect that sort of behaviour from us Latins."

Lieutenant-General Peter Walls.

Major Ronald Francis Reid-Daly.

Super sleuth Ken Flower, head of the CIO, and instigator of the Selous Scouts.

martial Nguni of South Africa, brought with them across the Limpopo River the higher sensibility and the military tactics of their Zulu forebears, which were then applied against the Mashona in a generation of brutal and bloody exploitation. The Mashona for their part were already a society in precipitous decline. In times past they had been one of the most advanced and enlightened cultures in sub-Saharan Africa, responsible for a commercial, cultural and social explosion on the central plateau that culminated in the construction and use of Great Zimbabwe as a political and economic centre. Thus it tended to be believed that the amaNdebele made a better fighting soldier than the Mashona who was viewed on the whole as friendly, passive and non-violent. Perhaps this was so at some point, but when pressed to the limit it was found that the traits of modern soldiering were common to both tribes. The black man, it was believed, tended to take a conventional view of warfare. He was, as a rule, an appalling shot, was innately terrified of heights and tended to lack the finest pitches of belligerence that usually made the difference in any aggressive contact.

It was these characteristics that Reid-Daly determined to drive out of his indigenous troops, and, according to his own accounts at least, he did achieve great improvements. The drop-out rate at this early stage was not high. This was perhaps thanks to the high quality of individuals initially attracted to the unit, but also perhaps because this first selection course was not as punishing as later versions would be. Despite this Reid-Daly was on the whole satisfied with the raw materials that he was left with. However, to challenge the courage and endurance of his men a little bit more, he devised a particularly cruel conclusion that certainly separated the men from the boys.

A concluding four-day endurance exercise was quite reasonably anticipated by most of the recruits to be the end of the ordeal. This would have stood to reason and no indication to the contrary was offered by the instructors. Most men accepted this fact and applied themselves to it. A cooked meal was promised to all at the end, and

indeed, as the ravenous men approached the finishing line the aroma of a lavish braai (barbecue) greeted them, along with hearty congratulations from the instructors that they had successfully completed the course. Then Reid-Daly himself arrived to address the haggard but jubilant assembly of men. As he opened his mouth to speak, however, the sound of a police Land Rover careening into camp caused him to pause. All eyes were then directed toward a local Special Branch officer as he climbed out of the Land Rover and hurried over to engage the commanding officer in a hushed but tense conversation. Reid-Daly then returned his attention to his men. With a knitted brow he addressed an officer in tones loud enough to be generally appreciated, revealing that a camp containing eight ZIPRA insurgents had been located on the Zambian lakeshore, and being the only available troops in the Kariba area, the new Selous Scouts were to be deployed on operations immediately. The plan was simple: the assault groups would immediately depart from Makuti to Kariba from where, under cover of darkness, they would cross the lake, mount the attack and return to Rhodesia before dawn, carrying with them what prisoners and documentation they had seized.

A carefully coordinated ruse then played out. The road journey took place, likewise a stealthy embarkation onto the District Commissioner's launch, followed by a covert journey across the lake. After a long and arcing voyage in pitch darkness the launch did not land in Zambia, but farther along the shoreline on the Rhodesian side. The assault groups, in full kit and ready for battle, were then told the truth. The selection truly was over.

There were those later who claimed that they had not been taken in, and certainly if anyone had glanced at the stars he might have pondered some navigational oddities, but on the whole the entire group received the news with surprise and a tangible outpouring of tension.

The party was held, the food eaten and the drink drunk, after which the first fellowship of the Selous Scouts stepped out into the world to do maximum damage.

CHAPTER TWO:
OPERATIONS COMMENCE

So much for the borrowed component of the Rhodesian counter-insurgency strategy. The home-grown ingredient was Fireforce.

As a pseudo reconnaissance formation the Selous Scouts were tasked with locating guerrilla groups within their operational areas, with a view to directing an airborne reaction force to take care of the business of killing or capturing them. In this way, and for long periods, Selous Scout groups were able to operate without compromising their cover. Fireforce was a rapid reaction technique which made use of a vertical envelopment strategy that, once perfected, became a vital factor in the success of the Selous Scouts, accounting for some 68 per cent of guerrillas killed within Rhodesia during the bush war.

Fireforce certainly was a formidable weapon. It comprised, in simple terms, a standby force located at various forward airfields scattered around the operational areas. It consisted typically of three Alouette III helicopters, or G-Cars, armed with door-mounted machine guns and configured primarily for troop deployment and support, and a fourth Alouette III, called a K-Car, which was armed with a formidable mounted 20mm cannon. This left room on board a K-Car for only the pilot, the gunner-technician and the Fireforce commander (usually an army major or captain). As of 1977, an additional complement of 16 to 20 paratroopers could be deployed from the venerable C-47 'Dakota' transporters. Air support was usually available from one of the Rhodesian air force's multi-functional Cessna 'Lynx' aircraft and a squadron of Hawker Hunters should all of this still prove inadequate.

The key to the success of Fireforce was speed, accuracy and aggression. The foremost proponents of the art were the RLI, although successful Fireforces were manned by members of the Rhodesian African Rifles, and later in the war by territorial units or independent companies. A notable example was 1 (Indep) Company which, during late 1978 and 1979, completed a hell-raising deployment to the *Tangent/Repulse* operational areas that put to rest most of the questions regarding the independent companies in the pecking order of achievement.

The successful symbiosis of the Selous Scouts and Fireforce was undeniable, and the strategy remained in deadly use until the war ended in 1980. In simple terms, a Selous Scout call-sign would be deployed covertly—initially by the device of debussing from a moving truck at night in order to give no hint to ever-vigilant local ZANU and ZAPU cell members that a deployment had taken place—after which the team would move either to an observation post (OP), normally situated on high ground, or into an insurgent operational area posing as an incoming group. The call-sign would typically include two white operatives who would remain largely in the background controlling events and doing what was described by Winston Hart as "the serious thinking".[8]

The black members, including the tame or turned element, would be involved in the liaison and mingling with the locals.

It ought to be noted here that the white pseudo operators in a team were often leanly provisioned; bearing in mind that the standard military system of ration packs could not be used under these circumstance. Quite a large part of the Special Branch role was to organize the supply of store-bought clothing and food, which would have been sourced from local trading stores, as well as their Warsaw Pact standard arms and equipment. As a rule, however, the pseudo groups were expected to survive off the resident population, as was standard guerrilla practice. The whites who could not attend beer drinks or political meetings usually had to subsist off what was brought back to them, which was seldom very much.

Once a suitable target had been identified the Selous Scout call-sign would repair to a safe location, typically on high ground with a visual command of the battlefield, from where details would be passed back to the regional Selous Scout fort out of which the group was operating. A detailed intelligence dossier would immediately be compiled by the Special Branch member working out of the fort. The air force would then be appraised of the sighting and a Fireforce placed on immediate standby. Once the decision had been made to scramble a Fireforce, pilots and ground forces, particularly the K-Car pilot, were given a detailed briefing from information supplied by the Scouts call-sign.

When the aircraft were ten minutes from the target area, the Selous Scout commander would begin to verbally guide the K-Car commander in by radio, precisely describing the terrain and highlighting any recognizable features that would aid navigation. Once the target had been identified the command helicopter would propel steeply upward from treetop level to a height of about 250 meters (or 800 feet above ground, the height at which the 20mm gun was calibrated), while the G-cars effected an anti-clockwise rotation of the contact area in order to pen the enemy in with mounted machine-gun fire. Once the Fireforce commander had taken stock of the situation and established the best troop drop-off positions the K-Car would commence an assault with its 20mm cannon. In the meanwhile, a Cessna Lynx, circling the contact area at a height of about 1,000 meters, would be available to engage the target with SNEB rockets, golf bombs or frantan, a locally produced napalm. Troops would be deployed in stop groups to engage guerrillas attempting to flee the scene. Paratroopers would be available if reinforcements were required, and if it was a large target, the attack would be preceded by a softening up by Hunter strike jets or Canberra bombers. As all this was underway the Selous Scout call-sign would monitor the contact and pass developing information on to the Fireforce

A Portuguese Alouette in action, Tete Province, Mozambique.

Dale Collett.

commander in the K-Car. (It should be added that the K-Car pilot was equally adept at controlling a Fireforce action as his army counterpart sitting next to him.)

Precisely in this way, on the morning of 24 February 1974, Lieutenant Dale Collett reported back to the Selous Scout operations room that he and his group had pinpointed a guerrilla camp in the Kandeya Tribal Trust Land, north of Mount Darwin. Reid-Daly immediately contacted the RLI Fireforce who were standing by at Mount Darwin and as daylight broke a formidable armada took to the air. From an elevated observation point overlooking the camp, Collett guided in the attack. The engagement was brief, clinical and ferocious. By 0900 six insurgents lay dead with another severely wounded.

This had been as clean and productive an operation as could have been hoped for and it was precisely the kind of vindication that Reid-Daly and his men had been working toward. Collett and his group, one of the original experimental teams, had deployed into the Kandeya TTL earlier in the week and within a very short time had succeeded in establishing their *bona fides* to the local contact man. This, again, very quickly led to the location of a genuine guerrilla camp. Following the Fireforce operation, a large haul of documentation and equipment was retrieved. What is more, the operation had handed the army its largest single body count so far in the *Hurricane* operational area, boosting army morale and solidifying the existence of the Selous Scouts.

Before long, Collett was out again with a fresh intelligence brief from Special Branch, and a strong interest in adding kills to that first spectacular success. In the early hours of 6 May news was once again returned to the operations room that Collett had located a guerrilla camp containing 20 insurgents. After a brief consultation with the Mount Darwin Fireforce commander, it was decided that an air strike would be put down before the

deployment of a heliborne RLI assault group to mop up any survivors. To mark the approach to the target Collett placed a fluorescent panel as close to the camp as he could, but in fact it was somewhat too close. At 0700 the air force went in but overshot the target, allowing most of the insurgents to escape the initial assault. Most did manage to flee, although the RLI claimed two insurgents killed in the ensuing follow-up with the addition of a live capture.

Later that month Collett was again reporting from Kandeya, this time of the presence of a large insurgent concentration. A Fireforce assault followed the next morning and within a few hours 19 insurgents out of an estimated 56 lay dead. Ten days later Stretch Franklin and his group, based up on the Ruya River, provided the intelligence for a Fireforce deployment that claimed another 26 insurgents. Fifty-two ZANLA insurgents had been accounted for in ten days. Many were wondering what on earth was going on. Nothing quite like this had ever happened before.

For the guerrilla units operating in the *Hurricane* operational area the impact of the Selous Scout deployments arrived like a hammer blow. Such losses of manpower and intelligence were clearly unsustainable. This prompted an urgent and thorough re-examination of guerrilla security protocols which took place throughout the entire command and control ladder. On the ground the foot soldiers of the revolution began to live in fear of the Selous Scouts, and indeed, of each other and the entire support structure that they depended on. The Selous Scouts were very quickly given the soubriquet Skuz'apo, an idiomatic wordplay in chiShona. The *skuz* was a bastardization of the English word 'excuse' or 'excuse me', and the *apo* meant 'here'. The implication of this was something along the lines of "Excuse me as I shake your hand and slip this knife between your ribs." There was some humour in it, but it was dark humour indeed.

For the pseudo teams on deployment the experience was both thrilling and highly charged. Group cohesion was judged on the whole to be good. The teams were typically made up of experienced

A C-47 Dakota lands at the old Mount Darwin dirt airstrip.

View from the door of a para-resupply C-47 Dakota.

men with freshly turned guerrillas, who were carefully watched until thoroughly compromised. This was usually deemed to have taken place once a turned guerrilla had scored a kill. Thereafter he could never hope to return to his old unit.

Despite this, turned guerrillas were usually armed men in the direct proximity of their erstwhile comrades, and no one could ever say for sure that a man had really turned. For a white team leader there was a race as well as an ideological contradiction in all of this. The principle of 'What do you mean *we*, white man?' has been disowned by every modern convention of race equality, but affirmative action has no place in the quantification of risk during war. This risk was obvious and present at all times, and each man knew it.

Only one incident has in fact been recorded of treachery in the field having fatal consequences. This was the deaths, in April 1975, of five members of a Selous Scout call-sign killed by a rogue member as they slept. The ease with which these men had been killed was an unavoidable risk of the necessary trust placed in the fundamentally unknown, and unknowable, quantity of captured guerrillas 'turned' and returned with their loyalty and intentions untested.

Haste was of course an essential part of the pseudo principle. The information available from a fresh capture needed to be acted upon quickly if it was to be effective. Usually it was essential that the identity of a recent capture be preserved both from local people in the vicinity of a contact and any security force personnel not involved in the business of turning him. The process typically began with courteous and concerned treatment, in particular if the individual happened to be wounded, in which case immediate and high-quality medical attention would be given. Bearing in mind that a man captured by the security forces had no reason to believe that he would not be summarily shot, or at the very least pushed through an unsympathetic judicial system that promised a hangman's noose at the end of it, such concern for his well being and the lavish care applied was an unexpected and pleasant surprise. Thereafter, it was customary for a wounded comrade

to be visited in hospital by an older turned guerrilla. The simple facts of the situation would be laid out and a rapport established, after which the eminent logic of switching sides in exchange for membership in the security forces, and the higher rates of Selous Scout pay, would be inescapable. It is worth noting that much of the individual Selous Scout income was drawn from the bounty system that applied to the regiment. Pseudo operators were paid Rh$150 for every guerrilla they killed or captured, or who was accounted for by the Fireforce actions that they were responsible for. All this presented a very tempting alternative to being handed over to the police.

Interrogation then followed. This also usually came as a pleasant surprise to the, by now, far more comfortable ex-guerrilla. The business would be concluded without violence or overt coercion, and since the capture was by now very eager to please, the onus tended to be placed on him to win the trust of his prospective call-sign. No Selous Scout call-sign was ever *ordered* to absorb a turned insurgent. They did so only on the basis of confidence and trust, and it was incumbent on the ex-guerrilla himself to provide that.

Once accepted, the man would soon find himself on deployment. This was the trickiest, but nonetheless, the most defining moment of the process. The willingness of a man to set up his friends and former comrades for capture or killing defined the extent of his commitment. Once a turned guerrilla had passed this rite of

A Selous Scout stick scrambles into action during a Fireforce contact in the Mtoko area of Operation *Hurricane*.

passage, the chances of him seeking to rejoin the revolution were almost zero. Having the blood of his erstwhile comrades on his hands was deemed sufficient proof that he had turned completely.

Another interesting strategy deployed by the Selous Scouts, partly as an act of humanity and partly to more deeply integrate the new recruit with his new support structure, was to uplift his family from the rural areas, should this be possible, and resettle them within the safety of the barracks at Inkomo. As mentioned, this served to protect them from any possibility of reprisals which, if they occurred, could be expected to be imbued with all the dark arts of African political vengeance.

Those arts had become a simple and brutal fact of life in the operational areas, and as such it presented the Selous Scouts with a unique conundrum. In the areas of population concentration in the northeast, ZANU had established what was, in effect, a parallel administration. This, although often invisible to whites, was of profound impact to blacks. Political malfeasance, real or perceived, against the revolution was responded to with the utmost brutality.

To illustrate this awful reality the Rhodesian Ministry of Information published a booklet in 1974 entitled *Anatomy of Terror*, which offered a short history of insurgent terror tactics during the period between 1972 and 1974. As much as it was a simple propaganda tool this publication was designed to illustrate to a world outraged by white intransigence in the matter of power-sharing, precisely who and what the Rhodesians were dealing with. Images of mutilated, burned, tortured and murdered human beings littered the pages. Such medieval methods of killing, as chilling and barbarous as they were, were nonetheless an almost

daily feature of insurgent justice and political enforcement in the rural areas. It was this that confronted the white youth of Rhodesia as increasingly more young men found themselves serving at 'the sharp end'. Most problematically, however, it was the popular expectation among local tribesmen that a similar style of justice and enforcement was being perpetrated by the Selous Scout teams as they sought to integrate.

In the aftermath of the war, and indeed during its latter phases, some of the most grotesque killings, atrocities and general abuses of human rights in Rhodesia were blamed by the Rhodesian government on the insurgent groups, and by the insurgent groups, in particular ZANLA, on the Selous Scouts. This was a difficult charge to deny, or prove, since the Selous Scouts made it their business to act and behave as authentic guerrilla groups, and charges that they engaged in atrocities for whatever propaganda value that might accrue, carried at least a ring of truth.

In fact, in the shady hinterland of pseudo operations, where Selous Scout teams operated often beyond recall, and in instances where the personnel involved were ex-guerrillas for whom such behaviour was inculcated by the training and indoctrination that they had received, it is conceivable that such activity did take place. If it did it was never sanctioned, never publically endorsed and certainly never institutionalized. An interesting comment was made by Ken Flower, Director-General of the CIO, and the midwife of the pseudo concept in Rhodesia, on the matter of the Selous Scouts:

> Certainly, the unit contained individuals who performed
> heroic feats and fought with the greatest honour and

An Alouette III G-Car coming into an LZ during a Fireforce action.

Colour Sergeant Clemence and Sergeant Dzingai practise hand signals during a tracking exercise.

A simulated (and realistic) contact during training. In the foreground are the 'guerrillas'.

distinction ... but it also attracted vainglorious extroverts and a few psychopathic killers.[9]

Like any other military unit and any other army, microcosms of the society they serve to protect, there was indeed a tiny nucleus of psychopathic killers in the Selous Scouts, and an informal internal process existed to excise what was deemed unacceptable within the ranks of the unit. This was the case within the ranks of the insurgent forces too, although institutionalized brutality was part and parcel of their *modus operandi*. Young men, often uneducated and intoxicated by the power of life and death they held over a terrified population, very frequently lapsed into indescribable violence. However, in the grossest incidences of this, individuals would be withdrawn from the field and dealt with according to their own codes of justice.

Of the vainglorious extroverts the world press and the detractors of the regiment closer to home had much to say. There can be no doubt that the Selous Scout Regiment fast-tracked its legend, and in doing so drew attention to itself in a manner most unbecoming of a covert reconnaissance unit in the special forces stable of any army. In fact, in the words of British historian and journalist David Caute, commenting in his 1983 book, *Under the Skin*, about the decline of white Rhodesia, the Selous Scouts were "upstarts in a hurry to describe themselves as legendary".

The Selous Scouts were an elite regiment, and bearing in mind that the legend has survived three decades beyond the existence of a regiment that was operational for a mere six years, there can be few who could effectively argue against that. Young men felt immensely proud of their association with this most maverick, unconventional and extraordinarily effective fighting force, and were apt at times to revel in it. Much criticism has been levelled at the Scouts for courting attention, despite their claim of operating in deeply covert circumstances. The famous Selous Scout beard was an example of this criticism.

The official history of the regiment, written by Colonel Ron Reid-Daly himself, states that the beard was adopted as a means of breaking up the features of the Anglo-Saxon face when confronted with the need to present white pseudo operators as black guerrillas. Others, however, among them Jim Parker, a member of the Special Branch Selous Scouts liaison group, felt that the beard was a badge of belonging that had little relevance in pseudo operations since blacks rarely wore beards. On the other hand, bearded men in uniform were instantly recognizable as members of Selous Scouts, and this, it has often been suggested, was the real reason they were worn, or at least became popular. As Jim Parker went on to note:

> Their highly successful external raids on guerrilla bases made the Scouts the public heroes of white Rhodesians. They lifted the spirits of the country which was in the grip of a demoralizing and protracted war that was taking its toll on the morale of the whites as well as some of the black population.[10]

Selous Scouts on follow-up.

Early days. Sergeant Bruce Fitzsimmons (back row, extreme left) and elements of 1 Troop, pose outside a tobacco barn on a Centenary farm, Operation *Hurricane*, 1974.

Selous Scouts at Wafa Wafa. Seated from left: Piet van der Riet, Charlie Krause, R.E. Beary, Chris Schulenburg, Martin Chikondo, Charlie Small, unknown; standing: unknown, Pete Clemence, unknown, Mick Hardy, Noel Robey, Willy Devine, Tim Callow and Steven Mpofu.

Anthony White gives a lesson on butchering an antelope

Willy van der Riet.

Meeting the Prime Minister. From left: Joe du Plooy (RLI, later killed in action on Operation *Uric*), Richard Passaportis (RLI, later Selous Scouts), Dale Collett (Selous Scouts), Stretch Franklin (Selous Scouts), Prime Minister Ian Smith, Ron Reid-Daly (Selous Scouts), Scotty McCormack (SAS) and Lieutenant Johnson (RLI).

This, needless to say, simply added to the general dislike and antipathy being generated by the Selous Scouts among those not involved with the regiment, and in particular those at the higher command level.

Another aspect of Selous Scout operational practice that caused endless irritation elsewhere in the army, but which was tactically essential, was the question of 'frozen areas'.

In simple terms this was the suspension of normal security force activity, and the removal of all orthodox units, from areas where Selous Scout teams were operating for the obvious reason of avoiding the sort of tragedy that had befallen Sergeant André Rabie. Ron Reid-Daly at that time was ranked as a major, and yet he was empowered beyond the normal protocols of military hierarchy to freeze extensive operational areas largely on his own recognizance, which was a source of no small irritation to the colonels and brigadiers commanding individual operational centres.

Despite all this, the Selous Scouts entered the ranks of the Rhodesian army special forces and scratched their mark on the tablet of military history. By the end of their second year of existence Rhodesia was deeply committed to war. All arms of the Rhodesian security forces experienced a rapid expansion with every able-bodied man and boy in one way or another involved with the armed services. Quite as the Selous Scouts solidified their reputation as a secret brotherhood of the shadows, a more overt and brazen arm of the regiment was delivering its first kicks in the womb of military necessity.

CHAPTER THREE:
EXTERNAL OPERATIONS—TERRORIZING THE TERRORISTS

Early in 1976 SAS commanding officer, Major Brian Robinson, and newly promoted Lieutenant-Colonel Ron Reid-Daly, were summoned before the Special Operations Committee to comment on the feasibility of mounting a raid on a large external guerrilla base situated in a heavily populated area of Mozambique. At the time little was known about the facility other than that it was situated on the west bank of the Nyadzonya River, a tributary of the Pungwe River, and that it contained a minimum of 800 enemy personnel. Two restrictions would be placed on the operation: firstly, there was to be a complete moratorium on air support except in the most critical circumstance, and secondly, the action must not be traceable to Rhodesia.

Both men examined the brief and reluctantly concluded that the operation was impossible. For the SAS a ban on air support would make a lightning entry and exit impossible, while for the Selous Scouts the likelihood of an overland infiltration and return, without running into serious trouble with either ZANLA or Frelimo, or very possibly both, seemed just too improbable and risky for the likely rewards.

The decision was a disappointment to both units. The SAS were the senior partners in the special forces stable, but the Selous Scouts were the up-and-comings with a powerful appetite to take the war to the enemy. Competition between the two lay submerged under a very thin veneer of commonality. The SAS had provided the formative personnel for the Selous Scouts, and certainly many more 'Supers' crossed over to the Scouts than vice versa. (So critical did this drain on manpower become for the SAS that Robinson was forced to take the matter up with Reid-Daly, who grudgingly agreed not to recruit further from the SAS.) The relationship was not healed at all as Reid-Daly began to make it known that he felt the Scouts were too ideally suited to the role of external operations for them to be excluded for long. And he was right.

The SAS was an elite regiment without a doubt. It enjoyed an august pedigree dating back to the Malayan insurgency of the 1950s, enhanced tremendously by its fraternal association with the iconic British SAS. It was the cutting edge of the Rhodesian strike capacity, backed up by the weight of the RLI, and in recent years used primarily on precision operations carried out in Mozambique.

The history of the SAS external operations in northern Mozambique in the early 1970s is really a history of the decline of Portuguese control of the territory. As with most of colonial Africa, black political agitation in Mozambique began in the late 1950s and developed into organized violence in the early 1960s. On 25 June 1962 the *Frente de Libertação de Moçambique*, or Frelimo, was founded as a broad-based guerrilla movement in opposition to Portuguese rule. The movement was briefly led by radical nationalist Eduardo Mondlane before his assassination in 1969. Thereafter it passed to the more aggressive control of the charismatic revolutionary Samora Machel, a one-time male nurse. The organization's rear bases were situated in Tanzania from where, with Soviet advice and support, it began to infiltrate insurgents into northern Mozambique.

As was the case in Rhodesia, the Zambezi River provided the Portuguese with a natural barrier that was reasonably easy to defend and which helped limit the insurgency to the north of the country and largely away from the more populated regions to the south. In theory this was fine, but in private the Rhodesians tended to be highly critical of the overall Portuguese security response and had very little confidence in the ability of the *Exército Português*, the Portuguese army, to contain the insurgency in the long term. There seemed on the whole to be much fire and fury in the Portuguese response but very little active engagement.

The matter was obviously of great significance and concern to Rhodesia. The likely effect on Rhodesian border security of Frelimo succeeding in breaching the Zambezi line and opening up fronts in the Tete and Sofala provinces was obvious. Land access to Rhodesia would, thereafter, very quickly become available to ZANU and ZAPU, which would in turn open up an extended front potentially stretching as far south as Inyanga and the Eastern Highlands.

In March 1968 Frelimo did indeed open up its Tete front in the four corners region adjoining Malawi, Zambia, Mozambique and Rhodesia. The following year the first SAS tracker team was deployed into Mozambique on a top-secret operation to proactively engage Frelimo. Militarily, the SAS was ideally suited to this type of work, but on the diplomatic front the matter needed to be handled extremely delicately. No suggestion was to be made on any level that the Portuguese actually *needed* this help. These were combined operations in the subtle military parlance of the moment. For Rhodesia it was simply a matter of doing what was necessary. Frelimo had not yet broached the Zambezi and the SAS was tasked with helping ensure that it did not.

Over the course of the next few years, SAS teams ranged extensively across northern Mozambique, operating at times right up to the borders of Malawi, Tanzania and Zambia. This was secretive, penetrating and demanding work which succeeded both in solidifying the reputation of the Rhodesian SAS and helping it develop the vital knowledge and battle experience that would be necessary to conduct later operations on a much larger scale and in far more critical circumstances.

Then Frelimo launched the 1970 offensive that did indeed drive it across the Zambezi near the current headwaters of the Cabora

Johne Fletcher shows off armourer Phil Morgan's converted RPD 1 for close-quarter fighting. The butt has been chopped off, the barrel shortened and the recoil feed mechanism reversed— something the Soviets were never able to achieve.

John Murphy, highly decorated ex-US Marine and Vietnam veteran.

John Murphy and Mick Hardy 'in the news' after the Mapai raid.

Operation *Mardon*. The Pig in action for the first time.

Rob Warracker sitting on the edge of a Pig during Operation *Mardon*.

Bassa dam. This was not only a decisive moment for the Portuguese defence of Mozambique but for the long protective line of white rule across the entire sub-continent. Effective control of a large swath of territory from the Zambezi River to the northeastern Rhodesian border was abruptly ceded to Frelimo. For Rhodesia the moment did not initially appear to be catastrophic—after all, Mozambique still remained substantively under Portuguese control, and the official Portuguese temper appeared determined that it should stay so—but it was nonetheless a source of growing concern.

From that point on external operations in the region increased in tempo as the SAS, in combination with the RLI, sought to keep Frelimo away from Rhodesia and to limit as much as possible the potential for ZANLA to piggy-back on Frelimo access and supply routes in the region.

One of the most important SAS external operations in Mozambique was that led by Lieutenant Bert Sasche in March 1972 in an attempt to establish the extent to which ZANLA elements were present alongside Frelimo in the Tete region. The attack on Matimbe Base in the Msengezi area yielded a number of kills and a large haul of documentation which indicated very strongly that formal cooperation between ZANLA and Frelimo had indeed begun.

As the front line in Mozambique now began to edge southward it began increasingly to envelop areas of greater population, which added to the ability of both ZANLA and Frelimo to operate, but which made it very difficult for white tracker or reconnaissance units to blend into the landscape. This, of course, was the signature strength of the Selous Scouts, and it offered space for the unit to start horning in on territory previously the preserve of the SAS (which refused to accept blacks into its ranks). As a reconnaissance unit it was once again becoming clear that the Selous Scouts might be capable of so much more than just the secretive work of internal pseudo operations.

None of this pleased the SAS which was not without some weapons of its own in this particular arsenal. The CIO was responsible for the establishment of the MNR (*Movimento Nacional da Resistência de Moçambique*), known also as Renamo (*Resistênicia Nacional Moçambicana*), which was trained and supported, and often used for external reconnaissance in Mozambique by the SAS. This did not help much in Zambia, however, where members of Renamo would be as conspicuous in the countryside as a white man, and it was not long before a request was submitted to the Selous Scouts by the CIO for the loan of black troops for the purpose of conducting reconnaissance work in Zambia.

It is worth mentioning here that Ron Reid-Daly was an early subscriber to a growing school of thought in the Rhodesian

Bert Sachse standing on a Unimog during Operation *Virile*.

Unimog with home-made mounted SNEB and armour-piercing rocket launcher.

Operation *Aztec*. The flying column near Malvernia. On the right runs the Maputo–Malvernia railway line, 120 kilometres of which was destroyed by the Selous Scouts.

Near Mapai during Operation *Aztec*.

security system that a more aggressive stance in the matter of taking the war to the enemy was necessary. Although it would be stretching a point to say that he was supported in this by the CIO Director-General, Ken Flower, it is true that Flower frequently made it known to the political leaders of Rhodesia that he also felt this to be a matter of urgent priority. Another of those in agreement was Minister of Defence P.K. van der Byl (1974–1976), a notable hawk in the Rhodesian cabinet.

The matter of taking the war to the enemy in any overt way, however, was something of a political minefield. The Portuguese would obviously be unable to countenance such a thing while they were still in power, while South Africa at the time was nurturing a surprisingly passive policy toward the seeping rot of black nationalism along its northern buffers.

Nonetheless the matter of attacking the insurgents at source remained in open discussion within the armed services which excited a great deal of informal debate. The political and military circumstances were at that early stage not in perfect alignment, but it did seem to many on the ground that some sort of regional

dimension to the war would occur sooner rather than later; in actual fact many were pushing for it.

Reid-Daly, in the meanwhile, declined to make available any Selous Scout personnel for external use, offering instead to conduct the reconnaissance as a Selous Scout operation. This was reluctantly agreed to and the operation went ahead. Of the two Selous Scout operatives involved, one was captured and subsequently disappeared, while the other only narrowly succeeded in making his way home. The episode was obviously an unmitigated disaster and, hardly surprisingly, fingers were pointed and blame assigned.

Reid-Daly's response was simply never to permit any of his men to take part in any operations that had not been planned by the Selous Scouts themselves. This, unfortunately, did nothing to heal the deepening rift between these "upstarts in a hurry to describe themselves as legendary" and the rest of the armed services. It can be argued that Reid-Daly had the best interests of his men at heart—there was never an instance where this was not true—but it also revealed something of his nature in being less concerned

Selous Scouts pose with captured Frelimo flag after the Mapai raid, 1976. General Walls (peaked cap) stands in the back row, left of centre.

at learning from his mistakes as disavowing them. Nonetheless, the Selous Scouts had effectively levered a crack in the door of external operations, a crack that they would work very hard over the next few years to open.

Meanwhile, events were taking place abroad that would pitch Rhodesia even more steeply toward a general insurgency and a further widening of the war effort. On 25 April 1974 a left-leaning military coup ousted the right-wing dictatorship of Portuguese Prime Minister, Marcelo Caetano. This event threw into immediate doubt the future of Portugal's overseas provinces, in particular Angola and Mozambique, both of which had been embroiled in costly and unpopular insurgency wars.

The Rhodesian public and body politic viewed these events with utter dismay. A promise made to its domestic audience by the new military leadership in Lisbon to end the African wars amounted in effect to a promise of surrender. What this would soon mean to Rhodesia would be a black, Marxist regime assuming power in Mozambique, a regime that could hardly be expected to be sympathetic to white Rhodesia and that in all likelihood would make its territory available for use by one or other, if not both of the Rhodesian liberation movements.

Mozambique achieved independence from Portugal on 25 June 1975. Within six months war had effectively come to eastern Rhodesia, opening a new front from the Zambezi River in the north to the Limpopo River in the south, some 600 miles of broken, vegetated and heavily populated country. The war was now on in earnest and within six months the first guerrilla incursions into the *Thrasher* and *Repulse* operational areas began to be felt.

In addition to this, a widely anticipated ramping-up of South African military support for Rhodesia did not take place. White Rhodesia was dismayed to discover that the South African Prime Minister, John Vorster, far from now seeing the inevitability of directly reinforcing Rhodesia, offered the country as a goodwill gesture to black Africa in a quixotic scheme to build an African commonwealth with South Africa at the centre. This was a policy the South Africans called *Détente*. Under South African pressure the leading black nationalists were released from Rhodesian prisons, a ceasefire was declared, and with its dependence on South Africa now absolute, Rhodesia had no choice but to indulge

Pretoria in a farcical foreign policy adventure that held out absolutely no prospects for success.

For Rhodesian military resources in general, all this meant a radical increase in both territorial and national-service commitments and a thinner distribution of the security forces countrywide. The conduct of the war imperceptibly shifted from an optimistic belief that a military solution to the crisis was practical, to a containment strategy designed to maintain the status quo long enough for a political solution to be wrought.

As part of this containment strategy the concept of external raids began to gain increased traction. The idea developed of shifting the focus of the war away from the internal operational areas, which would be left largely to the territorial battalions and the independent companies to contain, while the elite combat units would be directed primarily toward pummelling ZANLA and ZIPRA external rear and forward base facilities. A possible beneficial side effect of this would be a clear message sent to the governments of Mozambique and Zambia that the human and economic cost of picking a fight with white Rhodesia would be very heavy indeed.

This, in many respects, was the moment that Reid-Daly had been waiting for. The Selous Scouts had been in existence for more than two years and had already achieved extraordinary results in the field. The silent, highly skilled pseudo work that had been taking place daily in the operational areas around Rhodesia continued, and continued to yield good results, but the Scouts, Reid-Daly persisted, were capable of so much more. The pseudo theory in and of itself perfectly suited the initial role established for the Selous Scouts, but the extraordinary success of the turned-guerrilla concept opened up greater possibilities, in particular in the field of external reconnaissance and intelligence gathering, but also in hit-and-run strikes against guerrilla installations externally and jitter attacks launched against communication lines and other soft targets.

There were very few outside the regiment interested in hearing about this. Even at that early stage the Selous Scouts had more enemies than friends. Ken Flower was increasingly to be found among these, and he was well placed in the command and control hierarchy to support his opinions. To his mind the Selous Scouts had been configured specifically as an internal pseudo

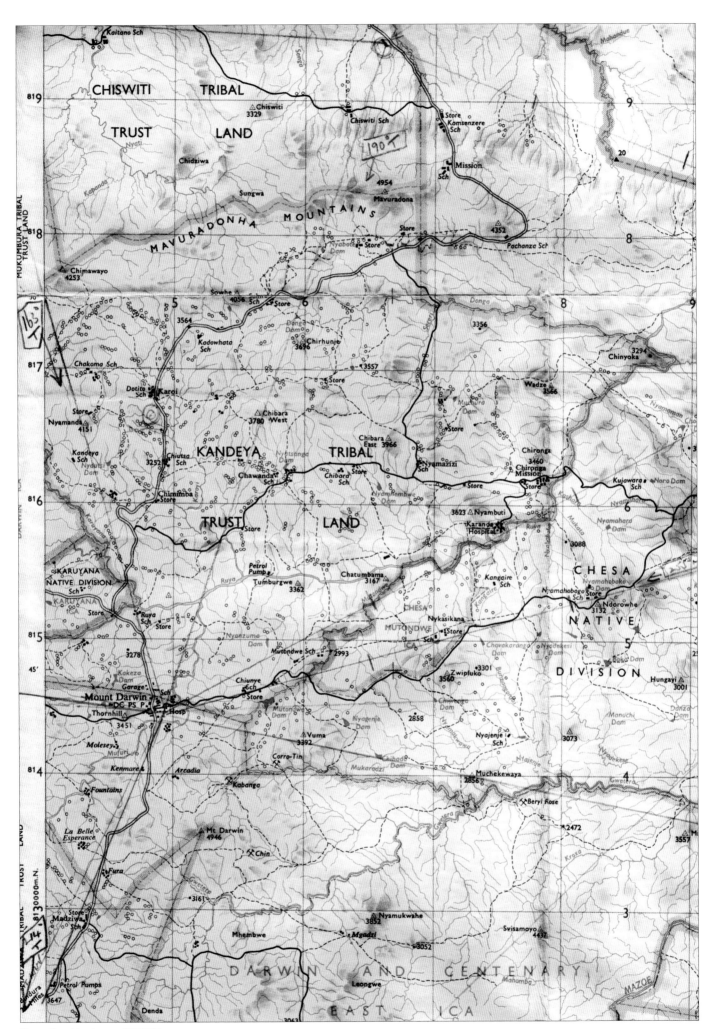

Operation *Hurricane*, 1972/73.

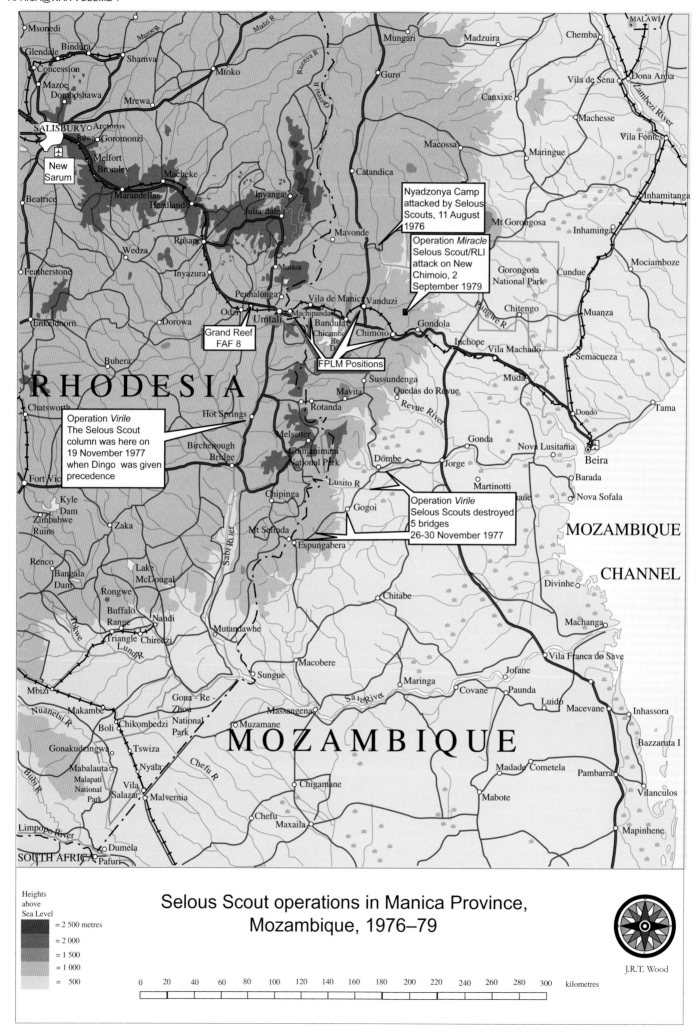

Nyadzonya Camp attacked by Selous Scouts, 11 August 1976

Operation *Miracle* Selous Scout/RLI attack on New Chimoio, 2 September 1979

Grand Reef FAF 8

FPLM Positions

Operation *Virile* The Selous Scout column was here on 19 November 1977 when Dingo was given precedence

Operation *Virile* Selous Scouts destroyed 5 bridges 26-30 November 1977

RHODESIA

MOZAMBIQUE

MOZAMBIQUE CHANNEL

Selous Scout operations in Manica Province, Mozambique, 1976–79

Heights above Sea Level

= 2 500 metres
= 2 000
= 1 500
= 1 000
= 500

0 20 40 60 80 100 120 140 160 180 200 220 240 260 280 300 kilometres

J.R.T. Wood

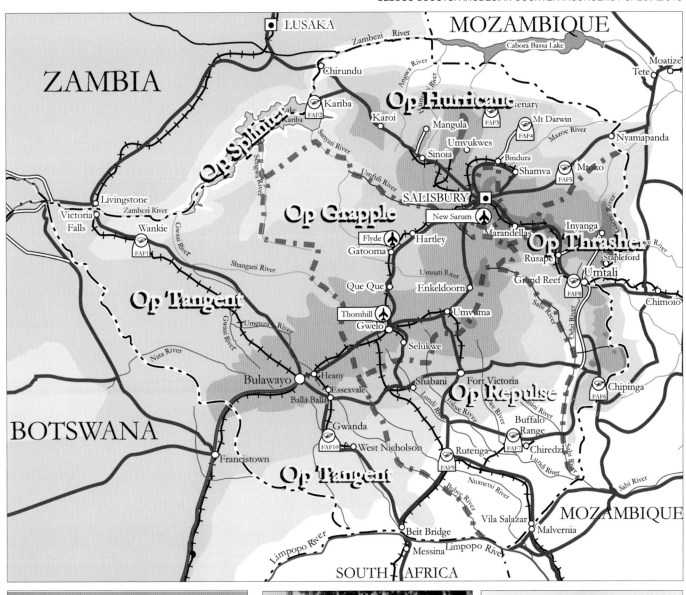

Piet van der Riet, Bronze Cross of Rhodesia.

Major Boet Swart.

Bruce Fitzsimmons.

Lieutenant Dale Collett, the country's first recipient of the Silver Cross of Rhodesia.

Charlie Krause, Bronze Cross of Rhodesia.

Neil Kriel, commander of the specialist Reconnaissance Troop.

A group of Selous Scout recruits during training.

Anthony White, seen here as a warrant officer.

Relieved recruits at the completion of an endurance exercise.

Captain Rob Warraker, Silver Cross of Rhodesia. Killed in action when the Canberra bomber, from which he was directing operations, was shot down over Mozambique. His body was never recovered.

Rabie, Franklin and Clemence.

Ron Reid-Daly on parade.

The Selous Scout Reconnaissance Troop, commanded by Captain Neil Kriel, poses outside Chris Schulenburg's pub, 'Tambuti Lodge', at André Rabie Barracks.

Selous Scout Recce Group, 1980. Back row from left: L/Cpl Letas, L/Cpl Madewe, Sgt Mudzingwa, Tpr Musiiwa, Sgt I. Waller, Sgt Mudhe, L/Cpl Norman, L/Cpl Francis, L/Cpl Tenga; middle row: Sgt R.A. Atkins, Tpr Charles, L/Col Bonga, Sgt Mlambo, L/Cpl Magama, L/Cpl Medu, Cpl Moyo, Tpr Ncube, Tpt Chiyaka, Cpl B. Thompson; seated: S/Sgt T. Fitzgerald, Lt E. Piringondo SCR, WOII W. Devine (CSM), Capt D.A. Samuels BCR (OC), Capt T.G. Bax (2IC), Capt T. Callow (OC B Tp), C/Sgt Zitha; front: Sgt M. RASH, Tps Carbon, Tpr Mapepeta, Cpl Pinos, Tpr Sibanda, L/Cpl Madiriza, Sgt Gibson.

Above: Selous Scouts prepare to board a C-47 Dakota transport.
Below: Operation *Miracle*, September/October 1979.

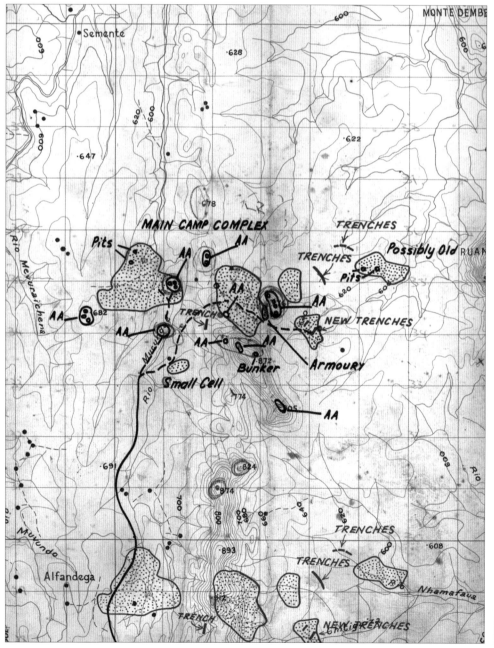

David Ndhlovu, Bronze Cross of Rhodesia.

Sergeant Mike Kerr, Bronze Cross of Rhodesia.

Peter McNeilage.

Right: Dennis Croukamp, Bronze Cross of Rhodesia, seen here in 1980 as an RLI warrant officer, having returned to his parent unit after the disbandment of the Selous Scouts.

A Fireforce operation: the view from the cockpit. *Photo: Jed Conan*

Operation *Miracle*. RLI armoured personnel carriers in the Honde Valley, en route to the Mozambican border. *Photo: Jed Conan*

Operation *Miracle*. The column crosses the Gairezi River, the border with Mozambique. *Photo: Jed Conan*. Below: Hawker Hunter.

Operation *Miracle*. In Mozambique, en route to the target. *Photo: Jed Conan*

Operation *Miracle*. Bell 205 resupply. *Photo: Jed Conan*

Operation *Miracle*. The ZANLA base burns. *Photo: Jed Conan*

Flying column infantry.

The Rhodesian air force bombards ZANLA's Madulo Pan base.

Richard Passaportis (dark T-shirt) poses on a heavily armed Pig with his crew.

An Alouette G-Car has just dropped a stick of troops as the ZANLA Madulo Pan base burns.

reconnaissance unit, making a clear point of avoiding the hunter/killer role, and it certainly was never intended that the regiment should be wielded as a fully constituted offensive force.

Reid-Daly, however, was still armed with close contact with the commander of the army, Peter Walls, and it was here that he aired his thoughts in preparation for the inevitable day that external operations would eclipse internal operations as the main pillar of war strategy.

With the fall of Mozambique, that day suddenly loomed large. Reid-Daly's first notable success was winning approval for an attack staged during March 1975 against an important ZANLA staging post situated south of Cabora Bassa dam at a place called Caponda. This was a relatively simple walk-in operation involving a small task force of some 20 men. The Scouts were warned once again, however, quite unequivocally, that there would be no authorization of air support should the operation run into trouble.

This was thanks to the on-again-off-again South African attitude to the war. Now that Rhodesia's access to the ports of Mozambique had effectively been cut off, Rhodesia found herself wholly dependent on South Africa for imports, exports, fuel, war matériel and direct military support. The *Détente* policy that had seen John Vorster dabbling with rapprochement in the lion's den of anti-white feeling in Africa had been devoured quite as one might have expected, leaving South Africa now abruptly aware that the *swart gevaar*, the black tide, had arrived at her border. Vorster now sought to deflect any sort of similar disaster in South West Africa, by joining forces with American super-statesman Henry Kissinger in finding a solution to the Rhodesian crisis.

Once again the Rhodesian Prime Minister, Ian Smith, was forced to bow to strangulating conditions placed on Rhodesian military aggression, while at the same time paying lip service to yet another frustrating bout of misdirected international diplomacy. The external deployment of air power to support Rhodesian troops probing east and north into enemy territory was one of these restrictions. It has never quite been established how many, but a number of the vitally important Alouette helicopters that sustained Rhodesian mobility were on loan from South Africa. Thus it was an extremely delicate political balancing act to keep her best and only friend happy, while at the same time maintain the momentum of war. It was an act that challenged both Rhodesian diplomatic and military competence to the limit.

In the meanwhile, the Selous Scout Caponda raid proved to be abortive, thanks to a cholera outbreak that had cleared the camp, consequently no attack took place. The operation was, however, more successfully repeated a year later.

Soon after, a second patrol was mounted into Mozambique, tasked with capturing a Frelimo commander in order to ascertain the current relationship between Frelimo and ZANLA. This operation resulted in an early casualty when a black Scout lost his foot after detonating an anti-personnel mine while crossing the *cordon sanitaire* between Rhodesia and Mozambique. However, the overall mission succeeded.

Meanwhile, the rapid expansion of the war resulted in the

Selous Scout flying column rampages through Gogoi, Mozambique.

Sergeant Rangarirayi, holder of both the Silver Cross and the Bronze Cross.

Corporal Pilate, Silver Cross of Rhodesia.

establishment of several new operational areas. Operation *Hurricane* remained in the northeast, with new areas opened up, including Operation *Thrasher*, stretching from Inyanga North to Chipinga; Operation *Repulse* from Chipinga to Beitbridge; and Operation *Tangent* from Beitbridge to Kariba. Kariba itself came under Operation *Splinter* and the Midlands under Operation *Grapple*.

Operation *Repulse* HQ was located at Chiredzi, where, in accordance with the organizational strategy of the Selous Scouts, a fort was established. From here internal pseudo operations were coordinated in the usual way.

However, interest began to be increasingly focused across the border in Mozambique, where conspicuous concentrations of both Frelimo and ZANLA were forming. There was also clear evidence, as there was in Manica Province, of cooperation between the two organizations, with ZANLA appearing to have full access to the local Frelimo transport and logistics infrastructure.

ZANLA combatants deployed into Rhodesia through this corridor usually made landfall at Maputo after training in Tanzania. Thereafter they were moved up to the border using the rail and road link that reached from the coast to the Rhodesian border. This rail corridor had been the same route used to ship sanctions-busted fuel from Lourenço Marques (Maputo) into Rhodesia, and now the same route was being used to move enemy forces into forward positions for infiltration into Rhodesia. This could hardly be viewed as anything less than an open invitation to the Rhodesian security forces to act.

Two railway settlements faced one another across the sealed border: Malvernia in Mozambique, named by Portuguese dictator António de Oliveira Salazar in honour of Rhodesian Prime Minister Godfrey Huggins, or Lord Malvern, who in turn named the opposing settlement on the Rhodesian side Vila Salazar. The former was occupied and heavily defended by units of Frelimo and the latter by the Rhodesian security forces. An ongoing hot war played out between these two positions, while back and forth across the border the Selous Scouts played an ongoing game of cat and mouse with Frelimo and ZANLA, attacking bases, compromising communications and generally doing what was politically and militarily possible to disrupt the free movement of the enemy.

The obvious target for the Selous Scouts was the transport infrastructure itself, and the various military facilities, staging points and bases associated with Frelimo and ZANLA. The first probing attacks in this area were launched soon after the establishment of the Selous Scout Chiredzi Fort. These were not spectacularly successful but they did serve to generate confidence and expertise, and helped to build a general picture of the lie of the land.

In 1976, the much admired Mercedes Benz Unimog 404/6 troop carrier and utility vehicle began to be introduced into service in Rhodesia. These robust and extremely versatile vehicles naturally excited the interest of the Selous Scouts, not least because someone noticed that they resembled very closely the 411 model that had been in wide use by the Portuguese in Mozambique and Angola. Many of these vehicles had recently been abandoned by the Portuguese and had passed into service under Frelimo, and were, at that time, a reasonably common sight on the roads of Mozambique. With a dab of paint and the addition of Frelimo number plates and insignia it seemed quite possible that the Rhodesian vehicles could be driven into Mozambique without raising any undue suspicions. The obvious potential of this for staging supported hit-and-run actions against the enemy was enormous.

It was decided to try out the idea. In May 1976, under the codename Operation *Detachment*, two ten-man teams using four disguised vehicles entered Mozambique with the limited objective of seeding mines and keeping a lookout for Frelimo or ZANLA captures of opportunity. The column penetrated some 100 miles inland using public highways without raising a hint of suspicion. Having arrived safely at its destination the column shot up the settlement, blew up a truck and scattered the area with mines before turning around and heading home.

Without doubt a great deal of interesting conversation accompanied the cold beers back at Chiredzi Fort that night. The most difficult aspect of planning a cross-border operation had always been the almost absolute freeze on the use of aircraft, a

Selous Scout mortar teams stand by in Gaza Province, Mozambique.

A Selous Scout flying column follows the Cabora Bassa powerlines.

John Murphy rests up during an external raid.

An air force resupply C-47 Dakota comes in to land at Mapai. A Dakota was later shot down here on take-off.

Goggled and bearded, a fearsome sight. This Unimog is mounted with .50-calibre Browning machine guns and a 20mm cannon.

limitation that had in equal measure a deployment, support and extraction ramification. And yet, if the concept of flying columns could be introduced into the picture, the range and scope of aggressive action in Mozambique could be dramatically increased.

And so it was. In June 1976, Operation *Long John* played out. This was a far more aggressive attack than at any time hitherto, aimed at the Mozambican settlements of Mapai and Chicualacuala. These two nominal towns were situated on the northern bank of the Limpopo River and both were home to large ZANLA transit facilities. The operation involved 58 Selous Scouts travelling in four trucks, with an additional two members dropped off in the contiguous South African Kruger National Park posing as tourists. From here the two slipped through the border fence and made their way overland the short distance to Mapai.

Chicualacuala was situated 20 miles inland from the Rhodesian border and Mapai 25 miles farther. The main target was Mapai and much peripheral damage was achieved en route before the column entered the ZANLA camp almost by invitation of a witless sentry. Once inside, sappers set about destroying 13 Mercedes Benz buses used to transport ZANLA guerrillas to the border. One bus was spared to transport captured armaments back to Rhodesia. What could not be hauled away was destroyed. Nineteen guerrillas were reported killed with another 18 wounded.

The death was also recorded of Selous Scout WOII Jannie Nel and the severe wounding of Lieutenant Dale Collett who was left paralyzed after being shot in the back.

One notable effect of this diversification of the Selous Scouts from pure pseudo operations was the increased need for more infantry-type soldiers, which resulted in a recruitment drive directed mainly at the territorial battalions of the Rhodesia Regiment.

The initial crop of territorials introduced into the regiment—those that had attracted a little of Reid-Daly's contempt—had by then won the respect of the regulars who, it must be said, could be guilty at times of a narrow field of vision. According to the late Captain Johne Fletcher: 'We ended up with an astonishing cross-section of the population, from the unemployed to chartered accountants, doctors, veterinarians, farmers, lawyers, tradesmen and one or two individuals with no visible means of support but who drove nice cars.'[11]

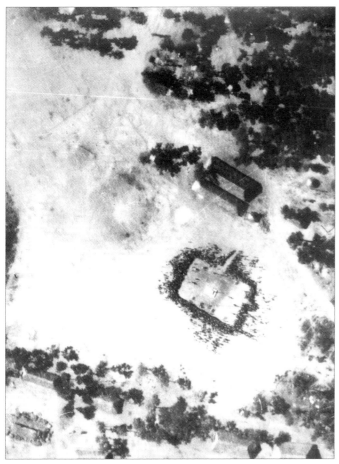

Aerial photograph, taken from a Canberra bomber piloted by Wing Commander Randy Durandt, of a muster parade at the Nyadzonya/Pungwe base before the raid. A count revealed over 800 ZANLA cadres on parade.

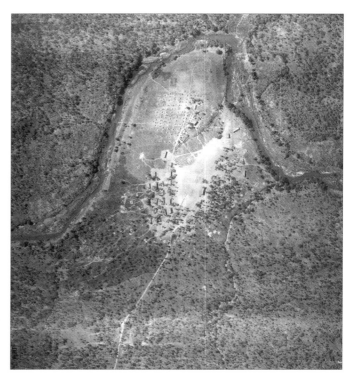

Aerial photograph of the Nyadzonya/Pungwe ZANLA base on a bend in the Nyadzonya River, Manica Province, Mozambique.

And by then, needless to say, Reid-Daly was himself willing to set matters straight:

> Once we had retrained and assimilated territorial men, and the scope of the regiment broadened to include external raids, they proved themselves top-class soldiers and carried out many fine operations both internally and externally. Indeed, in the hard years of the war which were to follow, I daily thanked my lucky stars for having the services of such fine fighting men, who performed so magnificently.[12]

The territorials brought an additional element to the Selous Scouts. These were not the acculturated 'white Africans' who made up the regular core of the unit, and were not, in the main, used on pseudo ops. They were orthodox infantrymen of an extremely high calibre who now made up the numbers on external operations. Being primarily civilians they introduced a range of diverse practical skills that regular soldiers often did not possess, and as a consequence enriched the blood of the regiment significantly.

Meanwhile, the unfortunate end of Operation *Long John* did not diminish the overall lesson learned, which was that the covert flying-column entry into Mozambique had real potential. It was then that the question of how to deal with the massive build-up underway at Nyadzonya began to generate renewed discussion. It would be an extremely daring feat to simply drive into Mozambique and attack a facility now believed to be housing 5,000 ZANLA combatants, and then turn around and drive home once the job was done, but practically speaking it was possible. Just the sheer audacity of it could quite conceivably carry it through. The superior qualities of the Rhodesian fighting man would level the odds somewhat, while the general state of disorganization and operational incompetence of Frelimo would offer a window of quick entry and exit if secrecy was maintained and the armed column was not immediately recognized.

The key to the success of an operation of this scale would be accurate and fresh intelligence. A fresh Selous Scout capture, Morrison Nyathi, claimed to have very recently passed through the camp. The information gained by a detailed interrogation of Nyathi brought the current picture of the Nyadzonya camp into much sharper focus and included a detailed description of the layout, command protocols and the fact that the camp contained mainly recruits who had been indifferently trained, were largely unarmed and were as a consequence unlikely to mount any kind of effective resistance. The primary risk lay not so much in a direct encounter with ZANLA but in getting out of Mozambique once Frelimo had been alerted to what was taking place.

Reid-Daly and his men spent a great deal of time considering every possible permutation of the operation but returned consistently to the notion of a flying column. This was the obvious and perhaps the only way to deliver sufficient force without the use of airpower. Moreover, the quickest and cleanest route to get there would be along the main roads and in through the front gate. Disguised as Frelimo and with a Portuguese-speaking detail capable of communicating with gate sentries, the odds were fair

A brave man: Morrison Nyathi, the 'turned' ZANLA guerrilla who played a pivotal role in the Nyadzonya/Pungwe raid that accounted for over 1,000 enemy deaths in August 1976. He was murdered by elements of ZANLA after Mugabe came to power in 1980.

ZANLA dead after the raid.

that the convoy could simply drive in. The question of firepower would be answered by a heavy complement of standard infantry weapons: the personal FN FAL assault rifles used by most Rhodesian soldiers and the FN MAG that served as the main Rhodesian infantry machine gun throughout the war, as well as a brace of 20mm cannons that had recently fallen into the lap of the Selous Scouts after the decommissioning of the well-serviced RhAF Vampire jets. These guns would each be mounted on the flatbed of a Unimog, and although somewhat *ad hoc*, would prove to be devastatingly effective. To back all this up a handful of the old British Ferret armoured cars equipped with their mounted Browning .303 machine guns would bring up the rear.

To achieve the element of surprise it would be essential to enter Mozambique undetected. While the column would make use of two of the region's principal roads, and pass through at least one key town, it would be necessary to find a route into the country that would not alert the Mozambican border control or Frelimo, and another out that would slip the noose of any ambushes or large-scale response organized by Frelimo in the aftermath.

It was left to Reid-Daly to sell the idea to the top brass, and this time it was not him but the Special Operations Committee showing signs of the jitters. This was partly due to the risk to men and equipment, but perhaps more so because the political process currently underway was moving toward all-party talks, scheduled to take place in October, and it would not have been politic at that moment to rock the boat. Reid-Daly, however, had the bit between his teeth. He exerted what pressure he could by making probably the most determined use of his direct line to General Walls than at any other time.

His logic to the army commander was simple. The matter could be delayed until the insurgents began to arrive in Rhodesia, in which case normal pseudo operations might in combination with Fireforce account for a majority of them at enormous military cost, or the job could be done in a couple of hours in concentrated form and at a fraction of the outlay. A short, swift, decisive blow could be delivered that might easily set ZANLA's military organization back years.

Walls was intrigued by the plan, but impressed too by the magnitude of the risk. He reminded Reid-Daly that all this would need to be achieved without air support beyond the casevac of only the severely wounded. Reid-Daly pressed the point, however, gaining the promise from Walls that if Rhodesian troops had their backs to the wall and were facing capture or annihilation, Hunters would be sent in. This was a minor concession but it meant a great deal to Reid-Daly. If the Selous Scouts became bogged down and were in deep trouble the Hunters might just be enough.

A few days later Reid-Daly was summoned to appear before the Operations Coordinating Committee, where he was questioned on the details of the proposed operation, and chided by a clearly irritated member for wasting time shortcutting the orthodox channels through his direct contact with General Walls. In his usual fashion, Reid-Daly no doubt shrugged this off.

The committee—comprising the Commissioner of Police, the

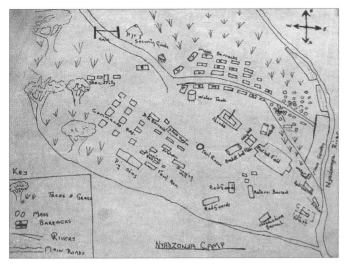

A ZANLA map of the base captured during the raid.

An aerial photograph after the raid. Hundreds of ZANLA corpses can be seen through a magnifying glass.

Commander of the Air Force, Lieutenant-General John Hickman deputizing for Lieutenant-General Walls, Ken Flower of the CIO, a representative of the Department of Foreign Affairs and the Chairman of the Special Operations Committee—entered discussions, and after several hours, and further questioning of Reid-Daly, the operation was cautiously given the go-ahead under the restrictions already outlined by Walls.

Thereafter, advance planning went into overdrive. The force earmarked for the attack comprised 84 men and 14 vehicles, including ten Unimogs and four Ferret armoured cars. These, as we have heard, were armed with mounted .303 Browning machine guns and were added to the overall arsenal against significant resistance from the Armoured Car Regiment. The Unimogs, meanwhile, were fitted with a battery of weapons including the ubiquitous FN MAG general-purpose machine guns in twin configuration, the menacing .50-calibre Browning machine gun, the 20mm cannon, a Soviet 12.7mm heavy machine gun, 81mm and 82mm mortars and the various infantry weapons carried by the crews.

The plan of attack was in principle very simple. The column would enter Mozambique under cover of darkness with both vehicles and manpower disguised to resemble a Frelimo detachment. It would use public roads to reach Nyadzonya where it would account for as many ZANLA combatants as possible, endeavouring also to capture what high-ranking personnel could be located before returning to Rhodesia by a different route.

The incoming route would essentially follow the main Umtali–Beria road through the border town of Vila de Manica before turning north onto the main road to Tete. This road crossed the Pungwe River over a substantial spanned bridge that would be destroyed once crossed to render impossible any sort of follow-up response from Frelimo detachments based in Chimoio and elsewhere. The main complication was the restriction on air power, but also of notable concern was the fact that the route into Nyadzonya plied through heavily populated areas which magnified the risk of the column being stopped or challenged by a Frelimo force. Should this happen the column could easily become isolated and destroyed, which would not only prove a

military catastrophe, but also a political disaster for both Rhodesia and South Africa.

Aware of all this Reid-Daly applied himself to exhaustively covering every possible eventuality. A mountain of intelligence was gathered and processed until a clear, three-dimensional picture of the objective had been built. The plan centred on the column entering Mozambique undetected, which required careful analysis of the various possible points of entry and with reconnaissance teams sent out in advance to test the feasibility of each. Secrecy was also key; should word seep out of what was afoot, the Selous Scout column might easily enter a waiting trap. Being massively outnumbered and heavily outgunned, this scenario, although it was in the back of everyone's mind, hardly bore thinking about.

The first vehicles quietly slipped into Mozambique at five minutes past midnight on Monday 9 August 1976, passing the first hurdle of a little-known smugglers' route into the country with just the loss of one Ferret armoured car to a driving mishap, and reaching the main EN6 trunk road that led from Forbes border post outside Umtali to Beira, without any major problems. The convoy then approached the sleeping town of Vila de Manica, taking care to circumnavigate the main avenues, and passing a Frelimo sentry box with nothing more than a desultory wave and a strong aroma of marijuana. So far so good. The road then left the town limits and headed out into the unlit countryside beyond. Soon the column reached the road junction with highway 102 that plied northward toward Vila Gouveia and Tete. The time was 0330 and all seemed well. Just east of the Pungwe Bridge the column pulled off the road to mark a little bit of time. Men slept briefly before first light when they began to move again.

A few miles farther on the turnoff to Nyadzonya was reached.

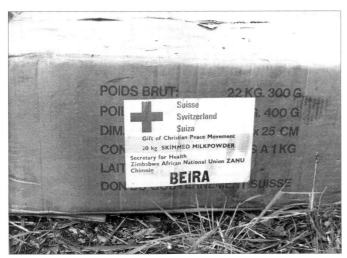

Support for ZANU/ZANLA came from a wide range of international aid and donor agencies.

Padre Grant addresses the troops at the memorial service for Captain Rob Warraker.

An ambush party comprising two Unimogs and 13 men stayed at the rear to cover the access while the remainder continued toward the target. Approaching the gates of the camp, the convoy, now comprising 72 men, gained access after a sharp command delivered in Portuguese to two credulous ZANLA guards who duly lifted the boom. As the trucks rolled into the camp the men riding in the flatbeds keenly observed the surrounding situation, most being astounded by the sheer numbers of ZANLA personnel mustered out in the open. The question in the minds of most, once the initial fear of a trap had been answered, was whether there would be enough ammunition to do the job.

Meanwhile, the infantry vehicles paused to drop off the mortar teams just inside the camp perimeter while the armed Ferrets peeled off to cover the anticipated escape routes. The main formation then came to a halt, upon which the Portuguese-speaking operative stood up and began to deliver a short speech. This was a lavish, slogan-rich proclamation of the fall of Rhodesia that was followed by an invitation to the comrades to gather around for more detailed news. This highly choreographed performance went ahead in front of a static but obviously intrigued audience of several thousands. The holiday of a day earlier had been extended and the general atmosphere of jubilation was electrified by the improbable news that the enemy had been defeated.

This vast human phalanx began to move forward and soon the vehicles were mobbed by cheering, ululating people. Clearly the population of the camp had no inkling whatsoever that this was a trap. There were a few among the milling crowd who were clearly in authority and were heaving their way through the crush in order to reach the vehicles, presumably to discover who they were and where they had come from. A black Selous Scout was shouting into a megaphone to try and regain some order over the chaotic noise of shouting, laughing, ululating and sloganeering. With nerves on edge the Scouts waited and watched as any plans that might have been formulated, for the moment, disintegrated into confusion.

Then, abruptly, fire was initiated. Elements in the crowd had identified a white soldier manning a machine gun and suddenly the tenor of the moment changed. The entire firearms complement of the attack force abruptly burst into life in a deafening but disciplined enfilade that cut through the massed ranks of humanity like a scythe. The dead mingled with the wounded, both trapping the living as they flailed for an avenue of escape from the sudden carnage.

From the trucks a steady and controlled fire was maintained. Spent shells rained down on the earth and piled up around the legs of the soldiers. The Ferrets that had been carefully positioned as stops along the presumed main escape routes mowed down those who attempted to flee. Others attempted to swim the Nyadzonya River and drowned. The thatched hospital building caught fire and burned to the ground with the sick and wounded still inside.

No significant resistance was registered. Fortune had played into the Rhodesian hands almost entirely. The column had succeeded in reaching the camp undetected, had found the occupants in huge numbers and in a festive mood, and in an action that required little skill or military precision, had wrought death on as many as came within range of their fire.

It was a simple, brilliantly executed and breathlessly daring escapade that did justice both to the skill of its architects and the unrelenting attention to detail that had been applied by Reid-Daly and his staff. Despite this, the operation did not conclude without a few complications. Once it had been established that such a gargantuan slaughter could hardly be disowned, air power was unleashed to free the departing convoy from an engagement with a large and supported Frelimo detachment. Thereafter, a rather scrambled overland rush for Rhodesia betrayed the nerves behind the ice-cold execution of the operation. On the whole, however, those that partook in it would have reached sanctuary with a few light injuries to report and an almost indigestible experience to collate and ponder.

Indeed, once the death toll had been reported it was revealed that some 1,028 cadres had perished that day. If the usual military tally of two wounded for every one killed were to be applied the bloodshed that occurred can then be fully appreciated. Rhodesia spared little effort and resource on the psychological rehabilitation of its troops, and no record has ever been made of those adrift in the Rhodesian diaspora who might have required it. It is hard to

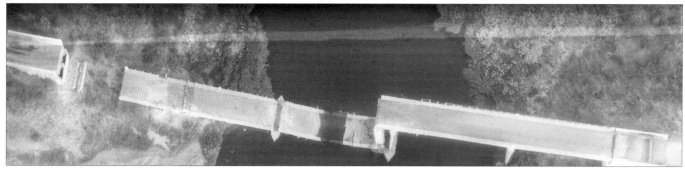

Aerial photograph of the Pungwe Bridge destroyed.

imagine, however, that those men who mounted their vehicles, with the smell of propellant and blood thick in the air, rode away from that scene that morning without having it revisit them in many forms for the remainder of their lives. War is hell, some say, and indeed it is.

This leads directly to the political and moral justification of the act. Was it justified? Was this indeed a military target?

Yes it was, although debate raged for years, and rages still. ZANU propaganda, for it was that, dominated the international press with pleas that a peaceful refugee establishment had been visited by the Rhodesian agents of death and such was the result. If women and children were involved, as indeed must have been the case, this was thanks in large measure to the villagization of guerrilla facilities in the time-honoured African fashion. If the United Nations made play of the fact that it was providing assistance to the facility as a registered refugee camp, then it had been fooled, and was in fact funding a military resource.

The incident also had precisely the anticipated political effect and Rhodesia was dragged over the coals by South Africa and loudly vilified by the international press. Internally, the likes of Ken Flower were shaking their heads in disgust. There may, he conceded, have been low-level training underway at Nyadzonya,

but in essence the attack had been a massacre of unarmed and scantily trained ZANLA personnel. The rift between Flower and the unit he had conceived widened to the extent that it could now never be repaired. A certain personal antipathy was also generated between him and Reid-Daly, resulting in an atmosphere of mistrust that also never healed.

An important consequence to this, one that would ramificate severely in the future, was the fact that Flower began from that moment on to distance himself from the Selous Scouts, in particular in the matter of swapping intelligence related to external operations carried out by the SAS and the CIO.

As a result, Special Branch Selous Scouts—not withstanding its links to the CIO—ceased to copy top-secret reports to the CIO Director-General, sending them only to Chief Superintendent Mac McGuiness.

For better or worse, however, the Selous Scouts were marked from that moment on as a force to be reckoned with. They were soldiers and the job they had been given to do had been done well. On behalf of a beleaguered people this small band of men had delivered a most bloody and painful punch into the face of the behemoth that let it be known in no uncertain terms that a fight with Rhodesia would be a fight indeed.

CHAPTER FOUR:
INTELLIGENCE AND THE RECONNAISSANCE TROOP

While the politicians dealt with the significant political fall-out of the raid, the Selous Scouts returned to Rhodesia and Inkomo Barracks to digest the stunning episode and evaluate the lessons learned. The flying-column tactic could not have proven its worth more spectacularly, as a consequence of which the Selous Scouts could now look forward to a lot more of this sort of work. How to make it work better became the next question. If the Scouts were now free to start attacking the enemy at source, how could the odds be improved?

The answer lay in better intelligence. Arguably one of the key pillars of the success of the Nyadzonya raid had been the exhaustive attention to intelligence detail that had provided a clear picture of what might be expected. By that point intelligence sharing between the various services had been more or less hamstrung by the growing partisanship and antipathy between the Selous Scouts

and others branches of the armed and intelligence services, which effectively meant that the Selous Scouts needed to develop more comprehensively their own intelligence structures.

This sorry state of affairs had, in fact, taken root very early in the life of the Selous Scouts. Reid-Daly had made a point of making available some of the unique information being unearthed by the early Selous Scout operations with a Special Branch member attached to Operation *Hurricane* in Centenary. This was not the run-of-the-mill intelligence that flowed in through the usual sources, but more peripheral, procedural material that to mainstream military planners might have seemed anecdotal. Included, however, were the names of Selous Scout contact men which proved to be a costly error. Armed with this information Special Branch rounded up all the named individuals for interrogation which blew the lid on a number of operations,

The Regimental Sergeant-Majors: WOIs Mavengere and Pretorius.

Padre Grant and the Colonel Reid-Daly discuss plans for the Selous Scout chapel.

The chapel nears completion. The CO's request to the World Council of Churches for assistance with funding to build the chapel was angrily ignored. (A WCC cheque had actually been made out, under the misapprehension that the regiment was a troop of Boy Scouts.)

endangering lives and setting back the process back many months. Reid-Daly was furious and promptly turned off the tap, after which not a scrap of intelligence was shared through direct channels with anybody other than those Special Branch details attached to and working with the Selous Scouts, known more or less from then on as Special Branch Selous Scouts.

An early recruit to this unit was Jim Parker, a Chiredzi farmer and police reservist. "Within 16 months of the formation of the Selous Scouts," Parkers states, "it became evident that major misunderstandings of the role of the unit—tempered by a degree of professional jealousy and aggravated by its top-secret nature— had caused rifts not only between the Scouts and normal army units but also between the Special Branch Selous Scouts and the police."[13]

These misunderstandings were unfortunate, but inevitable, and were enflamed at times by a very unseemly professional rivalry. In the matter of the handling of captures, the priority that was given to the Selous Scouts to cherry-pick who they wanted and promptly remove them from the remit of the correct authorities, irritated many within law enforcement. Unfortunately many of these people did not know that these captures were being turned and integrated into the Selous Scouts. The issue of frozen areas, another perennial bugbear in the system, annoyed many senior commanders and infuriated troops, but once again this was a matter that was not open to general explanation.

The net result of all this was the development of a system of in-house intelligence that was as watertight as it could be, and which, although it worked under peculiar circumstances, also generated much factionalism with a corresponding duplication of functions. Special Branch Selous Scouts, like its infantry counterpart, closed in on itself and became suspicious of outside influence. Jim Parker:

Although Special Branch as a whole fell under the control of the CIO, its liaison officers were often ostracized by their brother officers. The Commissioner of Police, Peter Allum, was top of the list of policemen who didn't like us. This was because we fell outside his control and although he was the most senior policeman in the country, he was

often not within our need-to-know loop. We also fended off jealousy-based actions that Lieutenant-Colonel Reid-Daly experienced from his brother officers. Then there was Ken Flower, Director-General of the CIO, who in the final months of Selous Scouts operations was cut out of our need-to-know loop as well. Although he was normally the Special Branch Selous Scouts's boss, it was felt he could no longer be trusted. Consequently, none of our top-secret briefings reached his desk. For his part Flower also kept intelligence away from us.[14]

Special Branch Selous Scouts evolved into a tight knit, independent clique, without which the Selous Scout pseudo operations would have been stillborn. SB Selous Scouts operational headquarters remained in Bindura, where the first Selous Scout installation had been established. The working relationship between these two principal arms of the Selous Scouts was smooth and effective. Every two weeks the liaison officers met for operational briefings at either Inkomo or Bindura. These meetings were usually chaired by Reid-Daly himself and were attended by army and Special Branch representatives from all the Selous Scout forts located in each operational area. Here operational planning and strategy were discussed.

A South African Security Police liaison officer was based permanently at the Bindura Fort, while a Rhodesian SB officer was assigned liaison duties with South African Military Intelligence and the South African Police Special Branch. South Africa was responsible for much of the SB Selous Scout vehicle complement and was known to provide special funds for Selous Scout operations.

As early as 1976 South African Reconnaissance Commando operators ('Recces') were embedded with the Selous Scouts, undergoing training in pseudo operations at the Selous Scout fort at Rusape. In 1977 the go-ahead was given by the South African Minister of Defence for the Recces to clandestinely assist Rhodesian security forces. These were formed into an *ad hoc* SAS squadron, D Squadron, which incidentally is featured on the Roll of Honour of the mother regiment, the British SAS.

It was rumoured that the informal Selous Scouts' patron was South African public relations and dirty tricks supremo Eschel Rhoodie, who slipped beneath the surface of South African secret operations after the Information Scandal, never to reappear. Much of the military and intelligence 'liaison' that took place between Rhodesia and South Africa was under the radar, often remaining undisclosed even to Prime Minister John Vorster and others in his cabinet. A certain amount of impropriety was suspected, and was probably inevitable, as a consequence of this anonymous to-ing and fro-ing between Rhodesia and South Africa. An investigation was attempted into the cross-border activities of Special Branch but little came of it. Various SB Selous Scout members had dockets opened or were investigated in one form or another by regular Special Branch members and the CID.

Despite all this, or perhaps because of it, Special Branch Selous Scouts remained an extremely versatile, flexible and effective branch of the service, the hand of which could be traced to the root of virtually every major Selous Scout success. They undertook the endless task of gathering and assessing the intelligence necessary for the deployment of pseudo teams or the establishment of observation points, and the intelligence that was returned as a consequence. The most important source of information available to SB was captured insurgents which included, for the most part, the detailed written records maintained by unit commanders in the field pertaining to orders, objectives, personnel and equipment. This information quite often included details of other guerrilla units in operation in any given area. Communications between insurgent sectorial commanders and their respective high commands were usually channelled back and forth through the use of young couriers or runners who were frequently intercepted or killed.

Information pertaining to any particular operational area was gathered, analyzed and pooled in comprehensive intelligence briefs that where delivered to call-signs operating or due to operate there. These briefs could, at times, take several hours to deliver. Up-to-the-minute information would have been vital, as would a detailed assessment of any area in terms of its deployments of guerrilla units, contact men and the key figures of any ZANLA cell structure. Upon the accuracy of these intelligence briefs the lives of pseudo operators depended.

As the Selous Scouts increasingly became a known fact in the countryside, the process of integration and authentication had become complex, elaborate and extremely dangerous. Guerrilla units regularly changed passwords, security protocols and systems of identification. These also varied between detachments. Go-betweens and contact men went in advance of every guerrilla detachment, testing the authenticity of strangers with extreme diligence, thanks to the likely interpretations and consequences of failure.

Needless to say, the lives of the pseudo operators hung very much in the balance as this process was underway. Counter-entrapment was always a risk, and it was as much a testimony to the diligence of the Special Branch Selous Scouts intelligence

Freefall course. Kneeling from left: Rich Stannard, John Early (instructor), Martin Chikondo; standing: unknown, R.E. Beary, Tim Callow, Piet van der Riet and Charlie Small.

Reconnaissance team in Mozambique.

acquisition and delivery as the teams themselves that their success rate was so high.

Reconnaissance work in one form or another was the key ingredient of all Selous Scout operations and the common denominator of both internal and external actions. This was the kind of work that the Selous Scout Regiment was perfectly configured to do. Men with the basic special force qualification of physical resilience, discipline and single mindedness of purpose had the added advantage of racial unity, forge-welded out of common experience and applied in a formula that was in many ways more than the sum total of its parts. The individuality that was so much part of the Rhodesian way of life was utilized but not adulterated, likewise the practical creativity and intuition common to the men who had created a nation like Rhodesia.

Field reconnaissance as distinct from pseudo operations was usually undertaken by sections of four or five men able to survive for long periods under operational conditions, often deep behind enemy lines and without outside support or the likelihood of uplift

'Wings' Wilson prepares to brew up.

Tim Callow, cross-border reconnaissance specialist.

should their situation turn bad. This formula worked well, but was improved upon considerably with the addition to the Selous Scouts in 1976 of one of the Rhodesian army's most august sons, Christofel Ferdinand 'Shulie' Schulenburg.

Schulenburg was a South African who had joined the Rhodesian army, as a number of South Africans and other foreign nationals did over the years, through a sense of adventure and the fact that the best action in the world at that time was arguably to be found in Rhodesia. Schulenburg served first with the RLI but in due course found a natural home in the SAS, as external operations in support of the Portuguese gained momentum, and it was during this period that he was awarded the Silver Cross of Rhodesia for gallantry on external operations.

On completion of his initial contract with the Rhodesian army, Schulenburg returned home to South Africa. In the meanwhile, the Selous Scouts had emerged as an elite, but somewhat less elitist special force unit than the SAS, but with much to prove and a lot of catching up to do. As Schulenburg languished in discontent south of the Limpopo, and as the war in Rhodesia intensified, news of the early experiments and successes of the Selous Scouts would no doubt have reached him. He and Reid-Daly knew one another, and were on good terms, but it was not until General Hickman tipped Reid-Daly off that Schulenburg was back in the country and looking for a new home in the army, that he learned that this celebrated reconnaissance supremo was back in circulation.

Initially Schulenburg approached his old *alumni*, the SAS, offering his services once again, but this time on very specific conditions. SAS Officer Commanding, Major Brian Robinson, had unsurprisingly been unable to accept this. It would, within the more orthodox structure of the SAS, have set a precedent which would probably have had a negative general effect. Reid-Daly, however, sensed immediately that the terms that the SAS had rejected might very well fit in with the emerging Selous Scout bag of tricks.

By then Schulenburg was already en route to visit Reid-Daly and when he appeared in front of the Selous Scout CO he did indeed have very clear terms for service. He wished to serve on a month-to-month basis and be removed from any troop-command responsibility. Furthermore, he wished to concentrate solely on

reconnaissance, operating alone, but with one colleague of his own approval should Reid-Daly insist.

Reid-Daly, tapping a pen between his fingers, and with a slight smile on his face, nodded as he digested all this. There were certainly plenty of advantages to be had using a one-man reconnaissance unit. Not least because a single set of tracks in the bush would not excite the kind of attention from insurgent units that evidence of a team of men on the move would. Covert movement and concealment would also be relatively easy, and since Schulenburg was prepared to offer the stern undertaking that he would never call in a 'hot extraction', the prospect was tempting.

However, regretfully, Reid-Daly shook his head. The risks of a one-man reconnaissance unit, particularly on external operations, were simply too high to consider. A three-man team could portage a wounded comrade. A two-man team provided the security of one man to kill the other in absolute extremis. But a one-man team was out of the question.

Those were the counter-terms that Reid-Daly put on the table, and Schulenburg agreed. Soon afterward, the whole business was sold to General Hickman whose only comment was to make sure that 'Shulie' was signed up as quickly as possible before he could change his mind.

Schulenburg did not change his mind. He was fast-tracked into the regiment with the rank of captain and let loose to test out his theories. It does seem that Schulenburg, upon entering into this arrangement, retained some of the SAS elitism with regards to the value of black troops in a special force role and their reliability in general. This, however, was a basic tenet of the Selous Scout *modus operandi* and he was by no means alone in having to consciously re-evaluate his attitude to operating alongside black troops.

He returned to Reid-Daly a short time later with the news that he had indeed come around to recognizing the key role that black operatives could make to a reconnaissance team. Although the key point was that black soldiers could mingle more easily in the rural environment, all the other aspects of black soldiering that were emerging to an appreciative white audience, and that stood out as unique in one form or another, served well the interests of subterfuge and concealment in the bush.

Chris Schulenburg takes off for an external reconnaissance operation.

Schulenburg's recce partner, Steven Mpofu ... Selous Scout extraordinaire.

Schulenburg.

Then came the question of deep penetration. Helicopters were obviously impractical for use in covert deployment in Mozambique, leaving parachuting as the only alternative. Schulenburg suggested, and in fact pioneered in the Rhodesian army, the HALO, or 'high altitude low opening' concept of precision parachuting. Reid-Daly seized upon the idea immediately and rushed off to secure air force backing. This was achieved with Reid-Daly's usual aptitude for getting things done and within a short time trials were underway.

Thus was formed the Selous Scout Reconnaissance Troop. The moment that Schulenburg appeared in the ranks of the regiment, and as the unique concept that he was developing became general, he found himself surrounded by similarly individualistic men of both races eager to get involved. Two-man reconnaissance teams soon became the standard operating procedure within the Reconnaissance Troop, while Schulenburg's unique and somewhat unorthodox views found a home among men increasingly fearless in matters of debunking established military theory and practice.

An early deployment of the two-man reconnaissance team took place in August 1976 along the Limpopo line, soon after the iconic Nyadzonya Raid, that returned information to Special Branch indicating that, after the destruction of ZANLA's bus fleet during Operation *Long John*, ZANLA had reverted to using the rail system in the Gaza Province to move men and equipment up to the border area for deployment into Rhodesia. Consequently the officer commanding the Selous Scout fort at Buffalo Range, Chiredzi, Major Bert Sachse, was tasked with attacking Frelimo's rail system between Barragem and Malvernia in an operation codenamed Operation *Prawn*.

Operation *Prawn* amounted to a series of probing attacks on the railway line, at first blowing small sections out of the line, which were all soon repaired, and later attempting to destroy larger sections. The operation did succeed to a large extent, but a proposal that it would culminate in the destruction of a large steel-span bridge to the north of Barragem was vetoed by the Operations Coordinating Committee as a consequence of concern over it being deemed an economic target.

A macabre example of Rhodesian inventiveness was displayed during this operation by the introduction of a recently killed ZANLA corpse dressed in Rhodesian camouflage and seeded with an impressive collection of bogus documents. This, when it was discovered, sent a Frelimo patrol quickly back to base to gloat over definitive evidence of Rhodesian involvement in the ongoing sabotage while a Selous Scout demolition team waiting nearby then simply moved forward and destroyed the line unmolested.

Despite these relentless attacks against the local rail infrastructure, and a great deal of general destruction besides, ZANLA insurgent groups were still deploying into the southeast of Rhodesia where the momentum of war continued to build. The Operation *Repulse* area was of significant importance to all three of the warring parties with ZANLA and ZIPRA squaring up in the region for local dominance and the Rhodesian security forces increasingly anxious that the vital road and rail links to South Africa remain open. The question of abandoning the access routes that ran through Gaza Province simply did not enter into ZANLA planning. The region would remain hotly contested and bitterly fought over right up until the closing stages of the war.

Operation *Mardon* took place over October and November 1976 in response to intelligence reports that ZANLA was preparing for a mass infiltration from external bases located in the Tete and Gaza provinces of Mozambique. The SAS, the RLI and the Grey's Scouts (mounted infantry) were tasked with attacking the numerous bases in Tete Province, while the Selous Scouts and 2 RAR were ordered to deal with the targets located within the Gaza Province.

Operation *Long John* of June that year had obliterated the ZANLA base at Mapai, and much of the town of Mapai itself, causing Frelimo to order ZANLA out of the immediate vicinity in an effort to try and put some distance between any potential Rhodesian attacks and the centres of civilian population. Consequently ZANLA relocated its camp closer to the line of rail at the junction town of Jorge do Limpopo. Guerrillas moved up by rail from Maputo were then shifted by road from Jorge do Limpopo via Maxaila and Chigamane to transit bases at Massangena. The part of the plan entrusted to the Selous Scouts was to mount flying-column attacks against Jorge do Limpopo, Chigamane and Massangena.

Captain Schulenburg is awarded the Grand Cross of Valour, one of only two recipients to receive Rhodesia's highest award for gallantry. On his right stand President Wrathall and General Hickman.

Alan Linder, the Intelligence Officer.

was attacked by a section of the column commanded by Lieutenant Richard Passaportis which claimed two guerrillas killed and a large haul of arms, ammunition, files and documents.[15]

The column returned to Rhodesia the following day without incident. The same, however, could not be said for the two reconnaissance teams. Due to poor weather both had been deployed a day later than scheduled and both had missed their designated drop zones. For Schulenburg and Mpofu the error was minimal and they were able to quickly re-orientate themselves and take up a position from where they could observe the road and railway line. Croukamp and his team, on the other hand, were dropped some 20 miles farther south along the railway line than intended and did not recognize the error as they laid their charges, cut the telephone line and took up their observation positions as planned.

After an uneventful night, Schulenburg and Mpofu, unaware that the column was now running behind schedule, began the day earmarked for the attack on Jorge do Limpopo by cutting the northward-probing telephone lines. Then, taking note of the fact that they were within a fairly densely populated area, decided to set up a diversion that would deflect attention from the main column which, they assumed, would be approaching the target area more or less at that time.

Schulenburg rigged up a claymore mine in a tree before both men deliberately made themselves visible to local villagers who were observing the pantomime from a safe distance with acute interest. Soon after, four men were seen hurrying off toward Jorge do Limpopo in order, it was assumed, to alert the local Frelimo detachment to the fact that Rhodesian soldiers were in the vicinity. In due course a Frelimo Land Rover travelling at speed, and bristling with armed troops, arrived on the scene. As it passed beneath the booby-trapped tree the mine was detonated with predictable effect on the unfortunate men travelling in the rear of the vehicle. The driver, however, appeared to survive, and despite careening wildly up the road, disappeared from sight.

Then, perhaps an hour or so later, the two Selous Scouts were surprised to observe a train arriving from the south, which paused at the nearby village and disgorged some 30 heavily armed Frelimo troops. These immediately dispersed and began to cast about for spoor.

The two Selous Scouts quietly gathered their equipment and set off in the opposite direction. No sooner had they done so, however, than they were greeted by the sound of a heavy vehicle moving toward them from the direction of Jorge do Limpopo. Working quickly, Schulenburg set up a second claymore which

The attack was precipitated by the deployment by parachute of two rearguard sections, one comprising Captain Schulenburg and Corporal Stephen Mpofu and another of three men comprising Sergeants Dennis Croukamp, Paul French and 'Wings' Wilson. These teams were deployed on the railway line on either side of the target to act as early warning in case the large Frelimo garrison at Barragem was mobilized to advance on the column. Schulenburg was also tasked to reconnoitre the base at Jorge do Limpopo in advance of the flying-column attack. Both teams would join the column on completion of the operation for a ride home.

In the early evening of 30 October the main pseudo column, commanded by Captain Rob Warraker, made its way into Mozambique. A gauntlet of brief ambushes by small Frelimo detachments was run, without notable incident, and the column arrived at Chigamane intact the following morning. Combined Frelimo and ZANLA resistance here was weak and was quickly suppressed. A respectable haul of documentation and equipment was collected before the column headed southwest for Maxaila, pressing on from there directly to Jorge do Limpopo.

On the outskirts of the town a support team armed with mortars was dropped off. Their plan was to fire directly over the heads of the advancing vehicles as they entered the town. The column, meanwhile, entered the settlement at high speed, surprising a troop train containing some 36 insurgents that immediately came under a withering storm of fire, causing it to halt and set ablaze. The Selous Scouts then spread out through the town, destroying a large water reservoir and the railway switching points, and setting alight any vehicles they encountered.

The following day the column, with the smoking remnants of an afternoon's work behind it, set out on the return journey to Massangena situated on the southern bank of the Sabi (Save) River, some 30 miles east of the Rhodesian border. Upon arrival, the column was warned by a friendly local villager that a Frelimo ambush lay in wait just outside of town alongside the airport. With this advanced knowledge the problem was dealt with reasonably easily. Thereafter, limited resistance was encountered as the column entered the settlement which was also dealt with without incident on the part of the Selous Scouts. A nearby ZANLA base was armed and detonated just in time. The blast ripped through a compact cluster of uniformed men, no doubt despatched from Jorge do Limpopo to assist in the search for the two Rhodesian soldiers. Later radio intercepts confirmed that this had been a large detachment of ZANLA personnel from the nearby Madulo Pan base.

If the objective of the two men had been to create a diversion then they certainly had succeeded. The immediate vicinity was suddenly alive with angry, vengeful enemy troops hard on their tracks. The two Scouts came under heavy and sustained attack from several sides and only narrowly, and, it must be said, with great composure and skill under pressure, managed to keep ahead of their pursuers. The sandveld conditions through which the chase was conducted very much favoured the pursuer with visible tracks almost impossible to obscure. The correct decision was made for the two to split up which confused and delayed the hot pursuit somewhat, but only somewhat, allowing both men to survive until nightfall which effectively brought the day's hectic action temporarily to a close.

By then plans were completely awry. In the midst of the chase Schulenburg had been able to raise the column commander, Rob Warracker, who was still en route to Jorge do Limpopo, but once the two men had split and the action had died down a little, Schulenburg was unable to make radio contact with anyone. The column had by then come within range of Jorge do Limpopo and could clearly hear Shulenburg and Mpofu under heavy fire but could do nothing to assist either man.

Meanwhile, a vehicle had been sent south to collect Croukamp and his three-man team but, after travelling much farther than it was thought the men would be, no sign of them was found and the vehicle returned. Similarly, after dark, a detached patrol was sent north in an effort to locate Schulenburg and Mpofu, but after no visible sign could be found, and no radio response returned, the patrol shot up an empty troop train before making its way back.

Warraker reluctantly concluded that the three-man team positioned south of Jorge do Limpopo had been either killed or captured and decided to pull out of the town that night in readiness for the advance on Massangena the following morning. Schulenburg, meanwhile, sat alone in the eerie silence of the African bush, happy to be alive, confident in his ability to survive, but deeply concerned about the fate of Mpofu whose whereabouts were unknown to him at that point. As he waited he became aware of the hum of an approaching aircraft. At 30,000 feet a Canberra was circling the target area in the hope of picking up a radio signal from the beleaguered teams. Back at Inkomo, Reid-Daly was anxiously waiting in his ops room for news.

Then, from the dark and unlit depths below, and to the commanding officer's inexpressible relief, Schulenburg's voice came softly over the radio. His batteries were all but exhausted though he was able in a short message to state his position and arrange a rendezvous for helicopter uplift at first light. At about the same time a hushed radio communication was received by Lieutenant Passaportis probing south along the main road in

search of the missing three-man team. Waterless for three days, Croukamp and his men had given up the column for lost and were no less relieved than any to be picked up and reported back safe to HQ.

The only member now unaccounted for was Mpofu. Schulenburg was cautiously uplifted the following morning under a barrage of enemy fire as the Frelimo detachment once again began its search for the two men. With the rising sun behind it the helicopter hung low to the tree line and skidded off back toward Rhodesia. It was a bittersweet moment for the Selous Scout reconnaissance supremo. He was on his way home but somewhere down there his partner was either dead or still evading capture.

Then, as the helicopter came in sight of the Rhodesian border, the pilot reported back to Schulenburg that he had spotted a figure on the railway line waving a white object. As the aircraft dropped lower, Schulenburg peered out and was able to confirm that this was indeed Corporal Mpofu. An extremely happy reunion took place in the tight confines of the Alouette after it had dropped to the ground, emplaned the relieved Selous Scout and quickly set off again.

Two weeks later Schulenburg and Mpofu were back in Mozambique, this time some 15 miles south of Jorge do Limpopo, concluding the business of Operation *Mardon*. The railway line in and around Jorge do Limpopo had been repaired by gangs working around the clock and once again trains were running between Barragem and Jorge do Limpopo. From there ZANLA insurgents were moved on foot to the Rhodesian border and deployed in-country.

Using pre-prepared demolition charges a speeding locomotive, the fourth thus far, was derailed and destroyed. This proved to be the last straw and no further use of the line was recorded until late in 1979 as the war was drawing to a conclusion.

Thus 1976 closed on an impressive Selous Scout scorecard. The 'armpits with eyeballs', as the Selous Scouts had come to be known by an appreciative public, had accounted for the killing of a known 1,257 enemy combatants and the removal from the ranks of a great many more, the destruction of untold quantities of arms and equipment, the destruction of millions of dollars' worth of enemy infrastructure and the acquisition of vast quantities of documentation and other intelligence material.

It is interesting to note that while internal pseudo operations fulfilled a vital function in the prosecution of the war on an ongoing basis, the achievements of this arm of the Selous Scouts were wholly eclipsed by the external operations. Of the kills achieved during this busy year only 181 were accounted for in internal operations. The original killer combination of the pseudo teams and Fireforce had now been superseded by the partnership of the highly effective Reconnaissance Troop, largely the brainchild of Captain Schulenburg, and the flying columns, which, all told, had accounted for most of the operational success thus far.

Quite how revolutionary Reid-Daly's concept was, particularly in introducing black special forces personnel to freefall parachuting, can only really be appreciated in the context of the times. It had been the race question fundamentally that was at the root of the political deadlock that in turn had brought about the war. Racial divisions in Rhodesia were almost absolute, and although to some degree this was loosened in the field of military service, nowhere was integration quite so comprehensive as it was in the Selous Scouts. The notion of a white recruit being berated by a black drill instructor, or a white trooper saluting and calling a black officer 'sir', was very difficult for many in the establishment to swallow. But for those who did, and only those,

the rewards of interdependence proved to be enriching rather than enervating. It was now increasingly widely appreciated that the methods of soldiering of men of equal wit, calibre, fitness and training differed only in style and not quality. It did not in any particular way influence mainstream society, since few probably even realized what went on behind the gates of a Selous Scout fort, but it was no less a unique and highly courageous experiment for that fact, particularly within an institution such as the army which is never comfortable with innovation or change.

CHAPTER FIVE:
THE SELOUS SCOUT SPIES

The successes of the Reconnaissance Troop caused Reid-Daly to consider developing the intelligence-gathering potential of the Selous Scouts further. Since Mozambique was a Portuguese-speaking country with an almost non-existent local white population, deep penetration into the country required covert entry and stealthy reconnaissance. Zambia, on the other hand, where ZIPRA military bases and command and control structures were largely centred, hosted a reasonably large rural and urban white population remaining in what was essentially an English-speaking country. Moreover, the country was a developing wildlife destination, so the movement of European tourists was commonplace. It stood to reason therefore, that more orthodox intelligence-gathering could be applied in Zambia with the infiltration of a white undercover agent.

The CIO in fact, whose preserve this type of operation was, did have an agent embedded in Lusaka and surrounds, who had since the mid-1970s been responsible for generating a great deal of mayhem in the capital, including the March 1975 assassination of ZANU political chairman Herbert Chitepo. Allan 'Taffy' Brice, an ex-British SAS soldier and an extremely able and dangerous operative, had remained undetected to the extent that, until the publication of his biography in 1985 by Rhodesian war historian Peter Stiff, there had been no clear evidence linking anyone with the assassination.

In this area of reconnaissance Reid-Daly felt that the Selous Scouts had a unique contribution to make. These, however, would be treacherous waters for him to enter, and he did so with caution, neglecting even to inform Mac McGuinness of what he had in mind. Rivalry within the intelligence community and the armed services, and in particular with regards to any aspect of Selous Scout activity, was by then extremely acute. There could be no clearer indication of this than the fact that Allan Brice was active—and very active indeed—in Zambia, but provided intelligence that was rarely if ever shared with Special Branch, and even more rarely still with Special Branch Selous Scouts. Reid-Daly would need to tread very carefully here, and indeed, initial friendly overtures to the CIO, promptly rebutted, tended to confirm this fact.

Captain Anthony White.   Lieutenant Chris Gough.

The Selous Scout CO, however, was not a man to be easily diverted. In his memoir he contents himself with the brief comment to the effect that a case needed to be made for the unique skills of the Selous Scouts, but in all probability it required a great deal more than that to get the ball rolling, possibly even another direct appeal to General Walls.

So far Reid-Daly had fought the good fight to get his regiment taken seriously in external operations, and in this he had been dramatically vindicated, and he clearly had no doubt that, given the opportunity, the Selous Scouts could do equal justice to this more conventional approach to intelligence-gathering.

It is perhaps worth mentioning here that the Operations Coordinating Committee and the national JOC had been superseded in March 1977 by a streamlined system of central planning known as Combined Operations (ComOps). This was headed by Walls who had been replaced as Army Commander by John Hickman. Responsibility for special forces was removed from the remit of the army and placed under the direct command of ComOps—General Walls in effect—with the army responsible only for logistics and administration. This move might have succeeded in streamlining the notoriously inefficient system of

Mike Borlace.

The corpulent Joshua Nkomo, ZAPU supremo.

ZANU chairman, Robert Gabriel Mugabe.

A series of deadly airstrikes delivered by the Rhodesian Hunters hit the camp on the morning of 19 October 1978. At that point the camp was believed to be housing upward of 3,000 ZIPRA personnel. The airstrikes were followed minutes later by a comprehensive series of bombing runs by the Rhodesian Canberra fleet, before being wrapped up by K-Car helicopter gunships armed with the deadly 20mm cannon. The attack itself, as dramatically successful as it was,

central coordination, but it did nothing to improve the relationship between the Selous Scouts and the rest of the armed services, serving above all else to highlight the cosy relationship that Reid-Daly was seen to enjoy with the now commander of Combined Operations.

Meanwhile, Reid-Daly made his first approach to Lieutenant Chris Gough with the idea of embedding an agent in Zambia. Gough was someone Reid-Daly knew well from an earlier period when both had served with the RLI, and who had the additional advantage of a Zambian passport. He was also, incidentally, a territorial officer. Gough was initially deployed to Zambia via Malawi toward the end of 1978, entering the country on a three-month tourist visa, time which he spent covering ground largely already covered by Allan Brice, but nonetheless establishing the fact at least that entry into and exit from Zambia was relatively easy.

His main focus of interest at that time was Westlands Farm, an old white agricultural property situated some 15 miles north of Lusaka, known otherwise as Freedom Camp, a ZIPRA facility that was also under the keen observation of the CIO. The location had been on the table as a possible external target for some time, with only the specific method of attack—either solely from the air or with the combined SAS/RLI airborne assault that had proved so devastating to ZANLA in Chimoio a year or more earlier—remaining under discussion.

The decision to mount an air raid on Westlands Farm had already been made at the highest level before Chris Gough made his reappearance at Inkomo, so much of the intelligence that the Selous Scouts had to offer had little bearing on the execution of the raid.

Soon after, the Rhodesians did indeed hit the ZIPRA Freedom Camp in another of those iconic moments that so enriched the brief history of the country. Nothing stirred the burdened spirits of white Rhodesia quite like these daring and audacious attacks, and this was one that would live for a very long time in the collective Rhodesian memory.

did not quite strike the heart of the nation as did the grounding of the Zambian air force by Squadron Leader Chris Dixon who announced to the control tower at Lusaka International Airport that any hint of hostile activity would be promptly dealt with. This was the iconic 'Green Leader' episode that so epitomized the Rhodesian approach to war, not unlike the early British South Africa Company Police efforts to seize Beira at the onset of the colony, and replete with the same engaging humour that was often to be found in the midst of all the slaughter.

On the ground Chris Gough was alerted to the fact that the attack had taken place only by the frenetic arrival in Lusaka of convoys of military and civilian vehicles ferrying the wounded to the University Hospital. Sensing an opportunity, he decided that the moment would be advantageous to visit the hospital for the sake of an anti-cholera vaccination that he had been instructed to have done upon entry into Zambia. Mingling in the chaos he was able to observe, unmolested, the result of the raid, thanks to which he was able to gain a fairly accurate sense of the number of casualties admitted. These he put at a figure in excess of some six hundred and fifty.

Gough remained in Lusaka for some weeks after the attack, gauging reaction, getting a sense of the rebuilding of ZIPRA forces at Westlands Farm and generally keeping himself busy. In due course he was recalled to Rhodesia.

In the meanwhile, events within Rhodesia reached a nadir when, on 3 September 1978, Air Rhodesia flight 825 was shot down by a surface-to-air missile soon after takeoff from Kariba. The aircraft crashed into a cultivated field, killing 38 of the 56 passengers on board with ten of the survivors being bayonetted and gunned down by a ZIPRA unit that arrived on the scene soon after. The Rhodesian public was shocked to the core by this event (which indirectly motivated the 'Green Leader' raid, or more correctly, Operation *Gatling*). Global reaction to the outrage was predictably muted, which served only to deepen the sense of isolation felt within the country. The feeling was magnified even further by ZAPU leader Joshua Nkomo, who responded with an amused chuckle on a BBC interview, admitting that his forces had indeed been responsible for the outrage.

The Rhodesian government had in fact been engaged in a love-hate relationship with the ZAPU leader, dating more or less from after his 1974 release from detention. Nkomo was seen in many quarters as the lesser of a number of political evils, particularly once Robert Mugabe had emerged as the leader of ZANU. If at least one of these hard-line nationalists was needed to authenticate any internal settlement, then rather it be Nkomo than Mugabe. Later, however, when Nkomo was proved complicit in the shooting down of flight 825, he began to be viewed with nothing less than vengeful wrath.

What to do about Nkomo in the aftermath was debated passionately at various levels of government. The decision to assassinate him was made, and in his most notable coup so far, the job was given to Reid-Daly and the Selous Scouts to take care of.

The first dirty puddle that Reid-Daly stepped into was in recognizing the fact that somewhere in the system there was a security leak. This fact, in the years since the onset of war, had become more or less established. The British undoubtedly had a mole in the CIO, and Ken Flower's name, rightly or wrongly, has often been suggested. That Reid-Daly suspected something like this at the time shows that he was a lot sharper than many people suspected. The fact that he sought to exclude a number of high-ranking military men, some exceeding him in rank, from the 'need to know' circle, irritated many of them. His relationship with Peter Walls was also in very conspicuous use at this time.

The operator chosen to undertake the mission was Lieutenant Anthony White, a well-seasoned Selous Scout with all the attributes of guile and courage a task such as this would require. Nkomo was known to be a slippery character and extremely alert to the risk of assassination. A year earlier his deputy, Jason Moyo, had been killed by a parcel bomb; in 1975 ZANU Chairman, Herbert Chitepo, had been obliterated in a car bomb explosion. With the Air Rhodesia atrocity so fresh in the minds of white Rhodesia, an attempt on his life would be almost inevitable. He was also notoriously fond of foreign travel and could be found junketing abroad as often as the ZAPU purse would allow.

It was decided that a radio-detonated car bomb would be the most suitable tool for the job. An appropriate model was located and adapted in the Selous Scout workshops before being transported north via Botswana. White was, in the meanwhile, furnished with a finely crafted cover and flown to Zambia from Johannesburg via Kenya, posing as a British taxidermist on the lookout for business opportunities in Zambia.

From the onset, however, the operation was dogged with bad luck. A comprehensive reconnaissance revealed that Nkomo was careful to select random routes and timings in his movements through Lusaka. Seven attempts to preposition the car bomb were thwarted, along with frustrating bouts of inactivity occasioned by Nkomo boarding an aircraft and disappearing for indeterminate periods. White began to run out of money, was anxious that he was beginning to attract attention and in the end opted to abandon the project, destroy the car and follow a pre-prepared extraction drill.

Even this was thwarted. He was required to make his way through the countryside to a location that would be under daily air surveillance by Rhodesian aircraft. Unfortunately, after walking some 30 miles through the bush, he began to suffer from symptoms of dysentery, complicated by encountering a native poacher who attempted to apprehend him, suspecting that a reward might accrue should he succeed. He did not succeed. After a short but vicious brawl the poacher was dead and White was left with no choice but to cautiously make his way back to Lusaka. From there he nervously boarded a scheduled flight and left the country.

Reid-Daly grasped the nettle and briefed ComOps on the failure. He assured the committee that the operation was still viable and was given a second bite of the apple.

This time Reid-Daly decided to augment the undercover-agent principle with something more in keeping with what the Selous Scouts did well. Another operative would be infiltrated into Zambia, but this time purely for the purpose of surveillance. Once it had been established that Nkomo was in residence, the killing blow would be struck by a conventional military assault mounted against his home.

The plan was simple. Surveillance would be kept on Nkomo's movements to establish his presence in Lusaka, while at the same time a suitable landing zone would be identified close to the capital from where an assault team would be helicoptered in for the purpose. The operative chosen for the task was Mike Borlace, an ex-Royal Air Force pilot and one of the more daring of a fearless breed of Rhodesian air force helicopter pilots. Borlace had sought a commission in the Selous Scouts in the hope of "interesting work", a request now about to be granted.

Interesting, in fact, would be an understatement. Borlace made his way to Zambia while an eight-man Selous Scout assault team led by Lieutenant Richard Passaportis went on standby at Karoi. A vehicle—a Land Rover, some might say a questionable choice if reliability is required—was chosen and customized for Borlace's use but before it could be sent up to him it broke down. A second vehicle, this time a Toyota Land Cruiser, was similarly customized and sent north, but was stopped at the Zambian–Botswanan border and turned around because the driver lacked a visa. A third attempt was made which at last succeeded. Borlace collected the vehicle in Lusaka after cooling his heels for two weeks and began in earnest to lay the foundation of the plan.

And then, to add to this catalogue of petty frustrations, Borlace began to run out of money. He was able to borrow locally but it all served to draw attention to himself, which was not in the least bit helpful. While reconnoitring a possible landing zone he ran into a Zambian military reserve and was detained briefly by a well-intentioned commanding officer who served him tea. Then Joshua Nkomo abruptly left the country, as was his habit, returning to Lusaka a few days later.

Now Nkomo was home, the message was relayed and that

Hickman and Reid-Daly take the salute.

A ZIPRA section, 1979.

evening two laden helicopters took off from a forward airfield in Karoi with the bristling eight-man attack force aboard.

Borlace, however, en route to the pre-arranged rendezvous, ran up against the obstacle of two washed-away bridges thanks to heavy seasonal rain and was unable to keep the appointment. For their part the Selous Scout assault force was landed in no less trouble. An accidental shooting resulted in the serious injury of one of the members, which required a second operative to stay with him while the remainder of the team pressed on. Their movement was constrained by heavy bush that had grown as was usual in the late season and the steady rain and mud that was a backdrop to it all. They arrived at the rendezvous but found it deserted. Shortly after, they and the wounded man were uplifted and returned to Karoi.

Back at Inkomo the plan was rehashed and two days later the Scouts were airborne once again. This time Borlace arrived at the rendezvous on cue but found no sign of the attack team. Passaportis and his men had become weighed down by wet seasonal conditions and arrived at the site only at first light. There, to their horror, they discovered that they had blundered right into the midst of a Zambian army exercise. They took cover as a Zambian army patrol came into view and stumbled on their tracks, radioing in immediately for backup. At this the Scouts wisely took to their heels. They managed to stay ahead of their pursuers, eventually outrunning them before being uplifted back to Karoi.

The whole episode began to appear surreal. The blacks said Nkomo had a *muti* stick that protected him from harm. Most of the white Scouts laughed at this, but there were some who did not. Whatever might be at the root of it, this was a devastating run of bad luck. For Borlace waiting at the 'sharp end' it was particularly unnerving. Each day his face became better known and his ongoing money problems were increasingly drawing attention to him as any one of a million possible scenarios of capture began to plague his mind.

Meanwhile, the plan was once again rehashed and simplified; the strategy was now to parachute onto a golf course adjacent to Nkomo's house, staging the attack and then navigating out of Lusaka on foot for a pre-planned rendezvous for a helicopter

uplift. Time, however, had run out. The attack force set off in the belly of a C-47 Dakota transporter ready to leap out over the metropolis and assassinate the ZAPU leader. Over Lusaka, however, there was no sign of Borlace. The mission aborted and returned to Rhodesia.

In the meanwhile, something had taken place that had convinced Borlace that it was time to leave. Reid-Daly received word from a fellow passenger on a scheduled flight that Borlace had been called in and detained by Zambian officials. A few days later the grim truth was confirmed: Borlace was in a Lusaka prison and could expect things to get very unpleasant, as indeed they did.

Reid-Daly and the rest of the Rhodesian high command were consternated. The Rhodesian security community was small, as was the Selous Scouts itself, and such things did not happen without it affecting the entire service. For Reid-Daly it was particularly bitter. His subsequent exchanges with ComOps and General Walls have never been recorded, but it is likely he was kept very busy putting out fires, as one attempt after another to free Borlace was aborted. This time, however, he was ordered to lend Lieutenant Anthony White to the Supers because the SAS had been given the job.

Not least, it was the wounded pride that stung the heart of both the commanding officer of the Selous Scouts and his regiment, aggravated by the crippling antipathy that had been generated against the unit over the last five hard-fought and glorious years of war. Reid-Daly lobbied hard and gallantly for a reversal of this decision, for clearly in his mind was a desire to get to Lusaka by one means or another in order to break Borlace out of prison. He pleaded with Walls the wholly impractical suggestion that the Scouts just fly in and be damned, do the job and get Mike Borlace out of there! Walls refused. Borlace, he said, had now to be considered a casualty of war. There was nothing that could be done but sit back and see how the Supers handled it. Theirs was a stylish scheme to land several Sabre Land Rovers on the Zambian side and drive to Lusaka, stage a strike against Nkomo's home and drive home. This they did with a high degree of precision. Nkomo's house was more or less demolished and a large number of ZIPRA personnel killed but Nkomo himself escaped.

This episode was one of the more intriguing enigmas of the war. Nkomo claimed that he had been in the house but had escaped through a toilet window. Analysts, which everybody in Rhodesia was at that time, dismissed the suggestion. The notion that the lumbering Nkomo, morbidly obese and barely capable of unassisted movement, might squeeze himself out of a toilet window in the midst of a ferocious firefight beggared belief. In all likelihood Nkomo had not been home, but had claimed a narrow escape in order to increase the dramatic effect.

Repeated attempts by Reid-Daly to find a way to rescue Borlace achieved nothing, with ultimately the events of the political endgame in Rhodesia overtaking the effort. Borlace was tried in a Zambian court and found guilty on a number of espionage charges and sentenced to a 25-year jail term. This was revisited by the Zambians in the afterglow of Zimbabwean independence, with the result that Borlace was released to return to Britain. By then, neither the Selous Scouts nor the nation they had served so well remained in existence.

CHAPTER SIX:
THE MUD BEGINS TO STICK

The fate of Mike Borlace weighed heavily on Reid-Daly and the Selous Scout Regiment in general. There was no clear indication of why, or how, he had been compromised but a possibility presented itself toward the end of January 1979. A Selous Scout signaller happened to be moving the telephones from Reid-Daly's office to a newly completed barracks and chanced upon a bugging device attached to a line that had been used, or so Reid-Daly claimed, to communicate with his Zambian agents.

In the customary manner of espionage and counter-espionage nothing was clear cut about this episode. Reid-Daly was understandably outraged and immediately sought to unearth who had been responsible. This certainly *could* have been at the root of Mike Borlace's exposure, but, as observed by political commentators Godwin and Hancock in the book *Rhodesians Never Die*: "Reid-Daly was incensed, claiming that a spy could have overheard his calls to an agent in Zambia, thereby admitting that he used an open line to communicate with his agents."[16]

In Reid-Daly's own account of Selous Scout operations, it is clear that communications had in fact been very carefully routed through an agent in South Africa who would have been the subject of any exchanges directed from the bugged telephone, and might, by those means, have compromised Mike Borlace. It is certainly not improbable. Reid-Daly, however, went on to observe:

> The situation in Rhodesia was crumbling. It had been crumbling visibly for at least a year. The stink of political defeat, which in practical terms always pre-empts a military defeat, even though the formations in the field might be intact and undefeated, had begun to seep like blood poisoning into the veins of the security forces, and even more visibly, into the veins of Rhodesia itself.[17]

And so it was. After 15-years of escalating war, six of which had been marked by the growing attenuation of the security forces against a backdrop of accelerating white emigration, Rhodesians at the higher command level had begun to turn on one another.

The bugging episode had its roots in mid-1978 when a disillusioned Selous Scout made the allegation that colleagues within the unit were freezing certain areas in order that organized elephant poaching could be conducted, the ivory from which, along with sundry captured weaponry, were being sold on to contacts in South Africa.

The question of illegal elephant poaching and the sale of captured weaponry has dogged the legacy of the Selous Scouts since the issue first arose. It is, however, to this day vehemently denied by the Selous Scouts Association and surviving members of the regiment. It must be remembered that two features of Selous Scout operational tactics—frozen areas and the harvesting of captured guerrilla weaponry, clothing and equipment for use by pseudo teams—created endless friction and animosity toward the Selous Scouts. Should a negative interpretation of these tactics be sought, it is not difficult to imagine that it would be said that the Selous Scouts froze certain areas for the purpose of poaching and accrued large amounts of captured equipment to sell on to other covert operators and collectors.

A version of the incident was offered by Jim Parker in his account of service in Special Branch Selous Scouts, *Assignment Selous Scouts*. During the early stages of Operation *Repulse* guerrilla units were making use of the settlement of Mavue, situated in Mozambique near the confluence of the Sabi and Lundi rivers, as a forward base. From here a well-known Mozambican elephant poacher by the name of Shadi (Shadrack) mounted regular hunting trips into the Gona re Zhou National Park. Somehow a Selous Scout Special Branch liaison officer by the name of Brian Sherry made contact with Shadi, and, without any official clearance or permission, offered the poacher free access to Gona re Zhou in exchange for information on ZANLA and Frelimo in the area. Involved also was a certain Jani Meyer, a local cattle rancher, professional hunter and territorial Selous Scout. Members of the Department of National Parks and Wildlife Management were also brought into the project for the purpose of authenticating the illegally acquired ivory.

It also so happened that late in 1976 Captain Chris Schulenburg and Sergeant Dennis Croukamp were involved in a deep-

Major John Duncan, OC 3 (Matabele) Group.

Colour Sergeant Ben Botha.

David Boyi, Bronze Cross of Rhodesia.

Colour Sergeant Andy Balaam MLM, a talented mortarman.

penetration reconnaissance in Mozambique when they were compromised by Frelimo and had to split up. Croukamp made his way overland back to Rhodesia, using the Limpopo as a landmark and arrived eventually at the Limpopo/Lundi confluence that marks the northeastern boundary of Gona re Zhou National Park. There he happened upon a Special Branch liaison officer from the Chiredzi Fort hunting elephant with an unknown black hunter.

Meanwhile, information was received by CID in Chiredzi from elements within the Department of National Parks and Wildlife Management that the Selous Scouts were indeed freezing areas in Gona re Zhou for the purpose of poaching ivory. Brian Sherry and Jani Meyer were arrested. It is worth stressing here, however, that had the illegal elephant hunting been an *official* Special Branch exercise, or sanctioned in any way by the powers that be, the actions of those responsible would have been condoned and any investigation halted by Mac McGuinness. Likewise, had it been a top-secret operation, no involvement by National Parks personnel would have been likely.[18]

The decision to investigate the Selous Scouts was taken by Hickman, then commander of the army, on the recommendation of the head of Military Intelligence, Lieutenant-Colonel John Redfern. Reid-Daly later claimed in an interview with Peter Godwin that this decision was taken because Military Intelligence believed that the CID investigating officer, Danny Stannard, who was a known friend of Reid-Daly, was involved in a cover-up. Stannard approached Reid-Daly with the allegations, let it be known that no personal slight was intended, but that an investigation was pending. Reid-Daly agreed, and was prepared to cooperate, letting it be known to his men that full cooperation was expected. A search was undertaken there and then, though no evidence of impropriety was unearthed. Stannard in fact ventured to add in his report that some evidence of professional jealously being behind the allegations was inescapable.

There may have been those in Military Intelligence who were not satisfied with this and who may have construed it as a cover-up but the fact remains that no firm evidence of institutionalized wrongdoing was ever unearthed. It is worth mentioning that

Parker claimed later, once his version of events had been published, that he received a death threat from ex-members of the Selous Scouts which might serve to imply that his assertions were either wholly fictional or wholly true.

According to Winston Hart, meanwhile, who was extremely close to Reid-Daly and who knew Hickman, Hickman probably did not realize upon issuing authorization to Colonel Redfern that it would involve the bugging of Reid-Daly's telephone. Hickman

Lance-Corporal Chigudu, Bronze Cross of Rhodesia.

at that time appeared to be grappling with a number of personal problems and might not have been as vigilant and judicial in the matter as he should have been. In fact the bugging when it happened was pursued without any great zeal and seemed to have been abandoned and forgotten about until a vigilant signalman noticed the device.

It was, however, the principle of the matter that angered Reid-Daly. He had once been very fond of Hickman, regarding him as one the best army officers he had ever worked under, and that it should have come to this! His anger was directed at Hickman who was showing visible signs of fraying at his emotional edges. After emerging drunk and almost naked from a car accident that occurred close to the official residence of the Prime Minister, Hickman found himself under an official cloud. In the midst of these problems, and against a backdrop of the crumbling political situation in Rhodesia and the breakup of his marriage, he was suddenly confronted by the Reid-Daly episode. He was successful in avoiding any direct contact with Reid-Daly until 31 January 1979 when the two met at a reunion dinner hosted by the Rhodesian Light Infantry to mark its 17th anniversary.

There Reid-Daly, later described as being emotional and overwrought, made an impromptu speech that was saturated with sarcasm, during which he thanked the army commander for bugging his telephone and remarked that if he ever saw Hickman again it would be too soon. Within moments the two were in heated argument and then squaring for a fight. They were pulled apart by colleagues, with Hickman loudly demanding that Reid-Daly be arrested for insubordination. Reid-Daly pointed the finger at Colonel Redfern, suggesting that he might at that moment be recording events in the mess, upon which the unfortunate Redfern was seized by the junior officers who dragged him into the billiards room and searched him. A hastily convened meeting of senior officers in the meanwhile concluded that Reid-Daly's behaviour did indeed justify a court martial, which could hardly have been avoided.

Before matters could proceed to that, however, Hickman left the country to holiday in South Africa, in an effort to clear his mind and repair his failing marriage. On his return he was summoned to appear at army headquarters where he was told by the Co-minister of Defence, Hillary Squires, that he had been dismissed from the army. This, Hickman not unjustifiably concluded, was a political manoeuvre, proving, in his mind at least, that the Reid-Daly episode had been a deliberate setup.

For his part, Reid-Daly demanded that action be taken against the officers responsible but recognized fairly early that within the general mood of defeatism prevalent in the army during those last months of Rhodesia's existence nothing was likely to be done about it. In reality, it hardly mattered. The writing was on the wall. The Rhodesian army had a matter of months to live. Against the backdrop of this, what possible importance could be attached to personal antipathies and perceived professional injustices?

Two days after the Cranborne Barracks incident, Reid-Daly was officially charged with insubordination to the army commander in contravention of the Defence Act. He, in turn, laid formal charges against eight officers for breaching Selous Scout security and endangering the lives of three of his officers—those who had

Lieutenant-Colonel Reid-Daly at the opening of the André Rabie Barracks. Mrs Rabie, André's mother, and General Hickman look on. With the so-called bugging scandal, Hickman and Reid-Daly were to become bitter enemies before war's end.

taken part in the Zambian spy ring. Soon after, he received formal notification from the new army commander, General Sandy MacLean, that no action would be pending against the eight.

Reid-Daly's court martial took place in June 1979 and lasted for five days, after which a guilty verdict was returned. In finding thus, Judge-Advocate-General Lieutenant-Colonel J.P. Reed expressed to the members of the court martial his abhorrence at the entire affair: "While having regard to the tenets of military discipline," he said, "your sentence will, I am confident, be a measure of your contempt and disgust towards this whole disgraceful bugging affair.'[19]

Reid-Daly was ultimately sentenced simply to a reprimand. In November 1979 he resigned his commission, handing over valedictory command of the Selous Scout Regiment to Lieutenant-Colonel Pat Armstrong, the recent 2IC of the RLI.

CHAPTER SEVEN: OPERATION *MIRACLE*

Whatever might have been taking place within the troubled high command of the Rhodesian army the war went on. The Lancaster House Conference opened on 10 September 1979 with the fate of Rhodesia balanced between the Patriotic Front (ZANU and ZAPU), headed by a belligerent and aggressive Robert Mugabe, and the government of Zimbabwe-Rhodesia led by a passive, anaemic and overawed Bishop Abel Muzorewa. The puppet master of the proceedings, Lord Peter Carrington, all things to all people, was determined by one means or another to bring a close to this long-festering wound on the face of the British colonial

legacy. Behind the scenes Samora Machel and Kenneth Kaunda fretted at the relentless battering being delivered to their national infrastructure by a weakened but still devastating Rhodesian army.

As the politicians, diplomats, journalists and dignitaries assembled in London to partake, observe or report upon this melancholy process, that brotherhood of war, the SAS and the Rhodesian Light Infantry, counting down the last days of their existence, took to the air again in Operation *Uric* to hit the Limpopo transport corridor one more time. During October 1979 the Zambian transport infrastructure was also attacked and

A flying column stick leader checks the route ahead.

A Willy's Jeep with a mounted Soviet 82mm B10 recoilless rifle ... and captured Frelimo flag.

Operation *Vodka*, a smaller 'external'. Selous Scouts advance on the ZIPRA base at Mboroma, Zambia.

Charlie Krause watches over two ZIPRA prisoners at Mboroma.

obliterated during Operation *Cheese*. SAS teams, with some Selous Scout and RLI involvement, calmly demolished most of the major bridges on all the major roads in the country.

All three units—the SAS, RLI and Selous Scouts—combined once again during September/October 1979 to mount what in real terms was as close as anything the Rhodesians had confronted so far to a conventional operation. Operation *Miracle* was also the last major hurrah of a fighting force whose sands were quickly draining.

Operation *Dingo* of two years earlier, perhaps the darkest moment in the war for ZANLA, had seen the obliteration of a significant insurgent staging camp and headquarters situated outside the Manica provincial capital of Chimoio. ZANLA suffered huge losses in this operation, reported to be as high as 3,000 killed and 5,000 wounded, which, notwithstanding the cannon-fodder mentality of the ZANLA leadership, represented an unsustainable blow. This prompted a re-evaluation of the design and construction of staging-camp facilities based on the assumption that concentrated formations simply invited Rhodesian attention.

Operation *Dingo*, meanwhile, had been executed with the loss of two Rhodesian lives. Those were the type of odds that the Rhodesians needed to keep abreast of the war. Anything that threatened more could not be considered viable.

By 1979, the Rhodesians had laid waste to a considerable weight of infrastructure in Mozambique and been responsible for the deaths of significant numbers of people, a large number of whom were not directly involved with the war. This was the high price of war with Rhodesia, a price that Frelimo was manifestly unwilling to continue paying. Strict rules now governed where and how ZANLA could operate in Mozambique. The location of a camp was to be well away from civilian areas, and in the event of attack, ZANLA personnel where to flee westward *into* Rhodesia, merging with affiliate tribes, and not eastward into Mozambique where the Rhodesians were bound to follow with the inevitable consequences.

All of this was precisely what the Rhodesian politicians wanted to hear. Mugabe and Nkomo were supported respectively by Samora Machel and Kenneth Kaunda, and it was known that each had warned his protégé that the war was unsustainable and must be ended at Lancaster House. Failing this, the faction leaders would be offered amnesty and no more.

This therefore was the strategic understanding as the Lancaster House Conference got underway, but behind the scenes both Mugabe and Nkomo recognized that boots on the ground in Rhodesia was what would make the difference in the general election that would be the likely outcome of Lancaster House. Thus preparations were underway to channel as many men as possible into Rhodesia in order to claim political space before any ceasefire could take effect. The Rhodesians, on the other hand, wanted to keep them out. Such was Operation *Miracle*.

It was clear from the rate of ZANLA infiltrations into the eastern districts of Rhodesia that significant activity was still taking place within the orbit of the old Chimoio camp. It was also known that administrative requirements necessitated that a reasonable proximity to Chimoio be maintained. Thus, although the Rhodesians were not able to pinpoint exactly where the new concentrations of ZANLA guerrillas were, they knew more or less where they were likely to be.

The first reconnaissance was undertaken by a combined SAS/MNR call-sign that was deployed into Mozambique by helicopter. It was quickly discovered, however, that the LZ was right within the complex that they had come to locate, which would later be shown to consist of a large number of individual camps distributed over some 40 square miles of well-defended territory. The reconnaissance devolved into a running firefight that continued until the team was narrowly uplifted by a hot extraction. With this in mind, the Selous Scouts deployed a two-man reconnaissance team on foot from Rhodesia, that was able to establish an observation post and gather some details of the layout of the complex. They were eventually intercepted by a group of female combatants and put to flight and likewise uplifted under fire by helicopter.

ZANLA was clearly bristling with the expectation that some sort of an attack on this facility was imminent. Despite the compromise of both reconnaissance teams, which should have been a clear indication that an attack was in the offing, the complex appeared to remain static. Even air reconnaissance did not prompt a hurried relocation of the camp. This led many in ComOps to suspect that the camp might well be a carefully laid trap. Intelligence sources had also indicated that Soviet advisers attached to Frelimo had been involved in expertly sited anti-aircraft defences around the complex. These could prove devastating to the dwindling assets of the Rhodesian air force just as large-scale infantry losses would be to the army. At that point in the war Rhodesia was balanced on a knife's edge and simply could not sustain significant losses of either personnel or equipment should the site prove to be a pre-prepared ambush.

Air reconnaissance, meanwhile, proved what was widely suspected. The complex was extensive and consisted on surface appearance of five distinctly separate camps, each well defended by heavy armaments and anti-aircraft emplacements sited among the boulders and rocks. The signature landscape of the Chimoio area—open woodland interspersed with domed granite kopjes, or *dwalas*—offered excellent defensive positions for the establishment of static defences such as this. This presented ComOps, somewhat reliant up until then on the standard Fireforce deployment for targets of this size, with something of a conundrum. Airborne troop deployments could very quickly become bogged down over a wide area with insufficient air capacity available to support and supply them. The target required something resembling a conventional attack which left a flying-column assault as the only viable option.

The Scouts were notified, at which point the project largely became theirs. This time, however, the column would need to be large and heavily reinforced. So late in the war, and with so much

Artillery Regiment armoured personnel carrier with 25 pounder in tow, en route to the Chimoio Circle.

Operation *Miracle*. Selous Scouts and RLI form up at Ruda in the Honde Valley, in preparation for the assault on the ZANLA base in the Chimoio Circle, Mozambique.

An armoured personnel carrier being towed across the Gairezi River into Mozambique. Serious delays occurred at the river crossing.

Artillery 25 pounders open up during the assault on the Chimoio hill feature that became known as 'Monte Cassino'.

Selous Scouts on top of Monte Cassino.

Two Selous Scouts try out for size the extensive ZANLA trench network at Monte Cassino. The devastation caused by the artillery and air bombardment can be seen in the background.

riding on the success of this attack, cooperation was forthcoming from every quarter. For additional firepower the Scouts requested the use of the Armoured Car Regiment's newly acquired Eland armoured cars. These were South African-manufactured reconnaissance vehicles modelled closely on the French Panhard AML, delivering a powerful punch from a mounted 90mm gun. The Rhodesian artillery provided a detachment of Ordnance QF 25-pounders that had been brought into service prior to the Second World War, and, as with most Rhodesian military assets, saw service long after they had been withdrawn from the front line of British and Commonwealth arsenals.

Extra troops, in the form of stop groups, for deployment along the eastern perimeter of the camp were provided by the RLI. These men would do steady work during the course of the operation as the bulk of the fleeing ZANLA guerrillas opted for an easterly departure from the scene of the fight rather than fleeing west, as ordered, into the waiting arms of the Selous Scouts.

The column, when it was finally assembled, was extensive. It comprised a number of infantry troop carriers and infantry-carrying armoured cars, interspersed with Eland armoured cars. The column commander, Captain Richard Passaportis, rode in a Pig armoured car, a Selous Scout innovation modelled on a West German APC and constructed around a Unimog chassis in the Selous Scout workshop. Although it profoundly lacked any pretence at aesthetics, the aptly named Pig proved itself in action on most of the Selous Scout flying-column attacks.

Unsatisfactory weather conditions delayed the start of the

operation which added to the jitters felt by the command element about security leaks, which in turn affected many of the troops who felt a growing sense of unease that perhaps ZANLA and Frelimo would be ready and waiting for them. When the weather cleared, and ComOps gave the go-ahead, the column crossed the Gairezi River in the Honde Valley and headed east into Mozambique.

Timings fell apart fairly early in the day. There was a rush to level the banks of the Gairezi and to firm up the riverbed to get the vehicles across. This had been left until roughly the moment of departure, for fear of alerting local tribesmen to the build-up of force and the potential for a Rhodesian attack. As a consequence the scheduled bombing runs were not supported by artillery as had been planned, for at that moment the old British 25-pounders were bogged down on the Rhodesian side, with the column in its entirety stretched out and fragmented over the length of the route.

As a result, ZANLA was warned hours in advance that the column was on its way, and that this time it was a big one. The incoming vehicles met low-level fire emanating from trenches that lined the access road. The first fatality, Trooper Gert O'Neill, was killed in a trench-clearing skirmish. It was late afternoon as the head of the main column arrived at the ZANLA base and dispersed to key positions around the complex where they dug in. For the remainder of the night they were subjected to harassing RPG-7 and 57mm recoilless-rifle fire, as well as regular and accurate bouts of mortar fire. There were no casualties but many close calls.

The sprawling character of the battlefield was simplified somewhat by the fact that its focus was a highly identifiable feature: a bald dome of granite running southeast to northwest with a wooded ridge at its rear. This imposing and rather forbidding feature was named for the purpose of this operation 'Monte Cassino', after the iconic monastic redoubt fought over in May 1944 during the battle of the same name in the Italian campaign. Monte Cassino offered its defenders a commanding field of fire, supported by smaller satellite positions, principally Hills 761 and 744.

It became evident as the sun rose on day two of the operation that a great deal of activity had been underway on the summit of Monte Cassino during the course of the night as the defenders shored up their fortifications. The steady ring of picks and shovels on hard rock had given clear indication that the 100 or so ZANLA regulars dug in on the summit were preparing to fight it out.

A Lynx spotter aircraft braved concentrated anti-aircraft fire to mark the heavily fortified Hill 761—known for the purpose as Ack Ack Hill—for the Hunters, which arrived shortly after and neutralized the position with deadly cargoes of 1,000lb golf bombs. Lieutenant Chris Gough—back from his tour of duty in Zambia—and his infantry troop of 27 Selous Scouts succeeded by 1500 that day in capturing Hill 774, from where he was able to effectively direct the mortar and artillery fire being concentrated on Monte Cassino.

No amount of this sort of attention, however, nor repeated bombing runs, was able to dislodge the defenders of the summit. It was decided at 1000 the following morning to mount an infantry

Passaportis on the radio from the back of a Pig.

An Eland 90 armoured car.

A baboon makes friends with his new master as the Scout tries to read his book after the battle for Monte Cassino. Baboons were used by ZANLA as early-warning sentries because of their acute hearing.

A Selous Scout prepares to demolish a bunker.

An exhausted Scout catches forty winks on the top of Monte Cassino.

A Bell 205 ('Huey') helicopter uplifts captured ZANLA ammunition from a cleared LZ.

Two soldiers take a break from loading captured enemy matériel onto helicopters to pose at the LZ

attack on the position. Behind an intense artillery bombardment two troops of Selous Scouts, supported by a 30-man RLI section, began the assault from the base of the hill. The unexpected return of a bunker bomb that had been tossed into a ZANLA trench almost had fatal consequences, but the exchange played out in the Scouts's favour and one fleeing guerrilla was taken down in a hail of gunfire. To quote Reid-Daly: "Rumours later said that he [the dead guerrilla] was white and had blue eyes, but he was an African. If he was a little white this can be explained by playing catch with bunker bombs."[20]

Bearing in mind that the hill was riddled with entrenchments the assumption was made that if one trench was occupied, all would be. Gough opted to avoid what would undoubtedly have been a long and bloody fight by sending the RLI and a small Selous Scout call-sign up the bald face of the kopje, while another Selous Scout call-sign plunged up the heavily defended western route, clearing the trenches as they went. Moments before the assault force bore down on the summit a barrage of mortar fire cleared the way. On arrival, the attackers found the position abandoned by the living. The relentless airborne, artillery and mortar barrages that had preceded the taking of the hill had left a battlefield reminiscent of Passchendaele. Pummelled vegetation, lingering smoke and a great many dead among the debris of hasty abandonment presented a melancholy picture. One RLI soldier was killed on the ascent with three others seriously wounded. It was reported shortly after that Ack Ack Hill had been taken, effectively bringing the operation to an end.

With the complex taken, a comprehensive assessment of what it represented was finally possible. Considering the size and extent of the camp, it was quite feasible that up to 10,000 guerrillas could have been housed and processed here. The camp had been heavily defended with a complex network of trenches that linked together a number of bunkers. Anti-aircraft emplacements were abundant, with the entire complex having about it a sense of military efficiency and orderliness.

In the meanwhile, and during the early hours of the following morning, an early-warning RLI call-sign manning a roadblock on the road leading in from Chimoio reported back to his commander that three Soviet tanks and a squad of Frelimo soldiers were advancing toward his position along the road. Artillery was promptly ranged and ten rounds were laid down among the advancing tanks. A second salvo knocked out the lead tank which halted the advance immediately. A dawn air reconnaissance identified the surviving tanks en route back toward Chimoio. Before an airstrike could be brought down against them, however, they had dispersed and gone under camouflage.

As the column withdrew, a Selous Scout call-sign stayed behind on high ground to monitor enemy activity. A day later it reported the arrival of a large Frelimo armoured column that accurately pummelled the vacant summit of Monte Cassino with Soviet-supplied anti-aircraft guns before turning around and leaving.

As a melancholy conclusion to the episode, it was believed that Frelimo would attempt some sort of reprisal attack in Rhodesia, so as to forestall this ComOps ordered a series of airstrikes. During the first of these a Canberra bomber was brought down by ground fire, killing both crew members. Then later a Hunter was brought down by ground fire, killing the pilot.

Engineers vehicle-recovery team poses next to a ZANLA troop-carrying Scania, captured during Operation *Miracle*.

Selous Scouts relax after Operation *Miracle*.

Above: Captured ZANLA weaponry and matériel: Soviet and Red Chinese armaments at Monte Cassino

Selous Scout armoured personnel carrier returns to Rhodesia with a captured ZANLA flag on the bumper.

CHAPTER EIGHT:
THE END

Carl Chibata, Bronze Cross of Rhodesia

Corporals Rangarirayi and Head Wuranda. Each held the Silver and Bronze Crosses and, as such, were the most highly decorated NCOs in the Rhodesian army.

Pfumo re Vanhu, or 'Spear of the People', auxiliaries. An ill-conceived idea to present so-called 'turned' or disaffected guerrillas to the outside world, these auxiliaries were, in the main, unemployed youths with no military training. Often in open revolt against their supposed master, the UANC, or worse, switching sides to ZANLA, they were a headache for the Rhodesians and easy prey for ZANLA who saw them as little more than 'sell-outs'.

Lord Peter Carrington and Bishop Abel Muzorewa of the UANC at Lancaster House. Carrington, in his haste to be rid of the 'Rhodesia problem', steamrolled through an agreement weighted heavily in Mugabe's favour, while Muzorewa let him.

Selous Scout Lieutenant Edward Piringondo, Silver Cross of Rhodesia. This legendary soldier was also nominated for the Grand Cross of Valour; however, the change of government in 1980 precluded the award. He was killed in action, February 1980.

When agreement among the warring parties was reached in London the war ended. There was a great deal of tension and misgiving manifest in the armed forces of Rhodesia as the process of peace began to unfold. A ceasefire was effected upon the provision that the Rhodesian security forces be withdrawn from the field and both guerrilla armies enter their forces into carefully positioned assembly points. With neither side willing to countenance the other assuming responsibility for security and law and order during the transition a small and somewhat symbolic force of Commonwealth monitors was assembled and flown out to Rhodesia.

In the meanwhile, for the first time since 1965, a British governor assumed authority over the colony in order to represent a return to legality and to preside over the transition to majority rule. Electioneering began with the first signature ceasefire violation being the false representation by their political leadership of guerrilla forces in the various assembly points. This permitted significant numbers of seasoned guerrillas on both sides of the liberation divide to remain at large in order to campaign on behalf of their leaders. By this stage in the war the cruel hand of guerrilla political enforcement had been felt throughout the country and in order not to rock the diplomatic boat combatants ranging through the rural areas merely had to remind villagers what was possible, pointing to the fact that the Rhodesian security forces were now nowhere to be seen.

Rhodesian whites had been assured by the British, and they clung to that guarantee that Robert Mugabe would *not* win the upcoming general election, most preferring to believe that a coalition of Nkomo and Muzorewa would emerge with a powerful white minority controlling the key institutions. An operation was devised, Operation *Quartz*, to unleash the Rhodesian security forces upon the ZANLA assembly points in order to forestall Mugabe's obvious reaction in the event of his losing the election, which would have been to return to war.

According to the terms of the ceasefire agreement all hostilities were expected to end at midnight on 28 December 1979. The moment that this announcement was made the Selous Scouts more or less ceased to exist, operating underground without central coordination, and attempting primarily to gauge black political opinion or to influence the electoral process through the use of pseudo gangs. Ceasefire violations were routinely blamed by ZANLA on the Selous Scouts, a tendency that continues to this day when on occasion uncomfortable evidence is unearthed of atrocities and human rights abuses committed at that time. The vast majority of ceasefire violations recorded were on the part of ZANLA, but the Rhodesians were certainly not supine.

How much of what took place during this closing chapter of the country's history was officially sanctioned and how much was not is difficult to say. In the absence of any other substantive white leadership General Walls became the public face of white Rhodesia. Behind him, however, was a military establishment in disarray, crumbling from defections and literally falling apart.

Between January and March 1980, the CIO, SAS and Selous Scouts made a number of earnest attempts to remove Mugabe from the picture. Special Branch Selous Scouts, with the technical assistance of the South African special forces, attempted to deploy a car bomb in Maputo as Mugabe and his entourage were en route to Rhodesia. When this failed a back-up plan was in place that involved CIO agent Allan Brice and four boosted TM46 landmines laid on the side of the road to be command-detonated as Mugabe's vehicle passed. This operation was called off without explanation.

CIO Director-General Ken Flower noted in his diary at this time that he had vetoed three separate assassination attempts on Mugabe scheduled to be carried out on the weekend of 2/3 February. One of these, no doubt, was the plan devised by the ever-resourceful Allan Brice to kill the ZANU leader by secreting a powerful command-detonated bomb in a culvert under the approach to his Mount Pleasant home in Salisbury. Once again, however, this plan was called off.

Thereafter things began to grow murky. *The Herald* of 5 February carried the story of an ambush staged against a private bus travelling between Salisbury and Umtali and carrying passengers believed to be supporters of Bishop Muzorewa and the UANC. Sixteen passengers, including women and children, were killed with many others injured. Combined Operations issued a communiqué blaming the incident on ZANLA guerrillas. A security force briefing held in Rusape the day after the incident heard the Special Branch Officer-in-Charge surmise that the single dead guerrilla found at the scene had died either from an accidental discharge of an RPG-7 or had been killed by his comrades after being seriously injured by the back blast of a rocket launch.

A very oblique reference to this incident is made by Ken Flower in his memoir that states: "In the event I managed to stop the original plans, but not the massacre of 15 or more wedding guests who should have played no part in this."[21]

According to Jim Parker, who conducted extensive interviews with, among others, Mac McGuinness, in preparation for his memoir *Assignment Selous Scouts*, the operation was carried out by a Selous Scout call-sign commanded by a Captain 'W', with Lieutenant 'G' and five other operators in support.[22] The objective had been to demonstrate that ZANLA had not ceased war operations and was continuing with attacks against its opposition elements. To help achieve realism a recently killed ZANLA guerrilla was removed from the mortuary and mutilated before being left at the scene. The effect was enhanced by planting a toothbrush and toothpaste of the type handed out by the Australian Monitoring Force soldiers to guerrillas at the nearby Assembly Point Echo. On the surface this seems unnecessarily elaborate but these were murky times indeed.

Soon after, yet another assassination plot against Mugabe was tried and failed. This time it was a combined SAS/Selous Scout operation in three parts. Plan A was to conceal a former Selous Scout—by then a South African agent—in an ambulance vehicle parked at Bulawayo airport and armed with a Soviet SAM-7 surface-to-air missile to shoot down Mugabe's aircraft as it came in to land. Plan B involved a ten-man SAS team ambushing Mugabe's motorcade as it left the airport en route for Bulawayo and Plan C involved a black Selous Scout who would pose as a journalist and place a microphone packed with explosive and ball bearings onto a speaker's podium where Mugabe was due to speak.

At the last minute the target was tipped off. Mugabe told Lord Soames later that he had heard that Nkomo was planning to assassinate him.

At 1355 on 10 February, Mugabe left an election rally at Mucheke Township in Fort Victoria heading for Umtali. Somewhere along the Fort Victoria–Umtali road a 40-kilogram bomb had been placed under a culvert. A command detonation missed the ZANU leader, and his deputy, Simon Muzenda, both of whom survived the blast.

Then a series of explosions occurred that appeared to target churches in and around Salisbury, incidents that were not immediately linked to a Renault 12 sedan that erupted in a huge explosion near St Mary's Anglican Church in the then Harare Township, killing the occupants and destroying the vehicle. A cheque book and vehicle registration document identified the owner of the vehicle, and one of two victims, as Selous Scout Lieutenant Edward Piringondo, recipient of the Silver Cross of Rhodesia and nominee for the Grand Cross of Valour, the highest Rhodesian award for bravery. Piringondo was later identified as one of eight Selous Scout members carrying out the attacks. One of the bombs had been a deliberate dud to leave clear evidence of its Soviet components.

Combined Operations issued an uninformative statement admitting only that the two fatalities in the vehicle explosion had been members of the security forces. In his memoir Ken Flower seems to shake his head at the blind lunacy of it all when he wrote: "Sadly, when I got home, I was again involved, in-or-out-of 'Special Operations', mostly unauthorized, half baked and more damaging to us than the enemy."

Mac McGuinness, when interviewed by Parker, stated that neither he nor ComOps had authorized the attack against the churches, claiming instead that the operation had been undertaken by "out-of-step Selous Scouts ... with their own agenda".

In reality, it was perhaps less a case of these men being out-of-step as re-aligned. The writing was on the wall as far as the Selous Scouts was concerned. The whites of the regiment had less to fear than the blacks who could look forward to meeting their erstwhile comrades in body or in spirit, and it was likely that the revolution would afford little clemency. Most whites in the Rhodesian special forces had the option to leave Rhodesia, and many did, thanks to an open invitation from the South African Recces offering a home to any that could adapt. Thus it could be construed that many involved were working on behalf of South Africa on the assumption that Rhodesia was by then well and truly a thing of the past.

Meanwhile, on 24 February 1980 a small group of Selous Scouts

Ceasefire, 1980. Joshua Nkomo chats with a somewhat bemused P.K. Allum (left), the Commissioner of Police.

Governor Soames, the last British administrator of the colony, arrives for his brief and emblematic sojourn in the country, Bulawayo, 1980.

and South African Recces broke into the Gwelo premises of the Catholic publication *Mambo Press*. A large explosive device was detonated that destroyed the printing press and killed a white male discovered to have had loose South African change in his trouser pocket. Another dead body was a planted guerrilla.

The attack on *Mambo Press* had been phase two of an earlier subterfuge that had seen a forged edition of the popular black-readership *Moto* magazine delivered onto the streets of Salisbury, featuring a purported psychological analysis of Mugabe that found him very wanting indeed. This had been an elaborate ruse and the attack on the printing press was a staged reprisal against it. It was by then more or less an open secret in Special Branch and

CID that South African special forces had been operating with elements—out of step or otherwise—of the Selous Scouts and the SAS for some time.

On 2 March 1980 the SAS made plans to shoot down a passenger airliner in which Robert Mugabe and 28 members of his entourage would be travelling. A SAM-7 would be used in the attack. Some sources, notably an account of the SAS, Barbara Cole's *The Elite*, state that the attack was called off at the last minute. Others suggest that the decision was made by the SAS operator himself, so as not to sacrifice the lives of other passengers on the aircraft simply for the sake of liquidating Mugabe.

Mugabe survived all these attempts to ultimately triumph at the polls. As voting ended on 3 March it was estimated that some 93 per cent of eligible voters had cast a ballot. Sixty-three per cent of those voted for Mugabe and his ZANU party. The entire hopeless charade suddenly crumbled and the worst of it was revealed. What might have been remained simply that and it was now too late to change anything.

The dissolution of the military system began almost immediately. Armour was withdrawn from the operational areas and returned to the home base of the Armoured Car Regiment, King George VI Barracks in Salisbury. The RAR companies filtered back to their individual home barracks while the RLI was withdrawn from the field and confined to Cranborne Barracks in Salisbury. The men of the Rhodesia Regiment and the rebadged RAR independent companies were all disarmed and sent home. Air force assets were withdrawn and returned to the main air force bases of New Sarum outside Salisbury and Thornhill outside Gwelo.

For all of the disbanded branches of the Rhodesian army some sort of commemoration and ceremony marked the end of their existence. Such was the case with the SAS and the RLI. Individual battalion events took place within the Rhodesia Regiment, offering the opportunity for an undefeated army to surrender its existence with dignity and due process. For the Selous Scouts, however, this was not to be. The loss of Lieutenant-Colonel Ron Reid-Daly as the father of the regiment, in the midst of a political implosion, and with all involved clearly able to appreciate what was imminent, precipitated a devolution of central command that could quite possibly explain much of the irregular activity that had so recently taken place.

By then many of the black members and ex-guerrillas had deserted, seeing with absolute certainty what lay in store for them. As Reid-Daly himself put it, some of the mud thrown at the regiment over the years had begun to stick. There was now a sudden rush to be dissociated with the regiment, so different from years past when Rhodesia idolized the Scouts and Rhodesian men clamoured to be allied with it.

Those who remained in the field were gathered together and returned to Inkomo Barracks. Regular members were ordered to remove their regimental badges and insignia and revert to those of their original parent unit. Territorial members simply went home, and thus the Selous Scouts simply ceased to exist.

EPILOGUE

There was some considerable irony on display as South Africa at last began to take note of what was taking place north of the Limpopo. There had been a similar expectation in Pretoria as elsewhere regarding the practical likelihood of Mugabe winning an outright majority, and there was no less consternation when he did. Of immediate concern, notwithstanding the wider geopolitical implications, was the effect that this would have on the hero-hungry black population of South Africa, restive for change and sensing the final defeat of white rule on the continent.

After prevaricating, throttling Rhodesia with ever more constraining terms and conditions, using the country as a pawn in its quixotic foreign policy experiments and offering crumbs of military assistance from a groaning table, it was now, as the chickens were coming home to roost, that South Africa finally reacted.

At the first meeting of the South African State Security Council after the election, Messina, the district opposing Beitbridge across the Limpopo River, was declared an SADF operational area. Plans were discussed for the assassination of both Robert Mugabe and president-in-waiting, Canaan Banana. The object of this would be to render the ZANU-PF government-in-waiting leaderless. The Rhodesian armed forces had been disbanded and would play no formal role in this plan but obviously hard-line ex-members would have been involved at many points.

The plan involved two key elements: the assassination of Mugabe as well as, incidentally, Prince Charles, who was attending the official handover as a representative of the British Crown, Lord Christopher Soames and his wife, and very possibly Lord Peter Carrington who would represent the British government. The operation was scheduled for 17 April, a few hours before the inauguration ceremony that would mark the birth of Zimbabwe.

The killings would be achieved by planting replica traffic-light control boxes at key intersections along the route that the official motorcade would travel between Government House in Salisbury and Meikles Hotel where an official reception was to be held. Meanwhile, a huge SADF battle group—Battle Group Charlie—would be poised at Messina ready to react the moment the order was given. It was anticipated that, as the news became general that Mugabe and other members of his entourage had been murdered, the broad assumption would be reached among the masses that it had been a white plot. A mass movement toward the northern suburbs would then culminate in the wholesale slaughter of the white population of the capital, a situation that would offer South Africa an acceptable diplomatic gateway and Battle Group Charlie would be ordered north to restore order and keep the peace until a more unilaterally acceptable solution could be devised. This would place South Africa effectively in the frame, a negotiating partner for any world power anxious to arrange a transition and

The Selous Scouts, a proud regiment.

a key player in deciding what the future face of a free Zimbabwe would look like.

The cost would be high: the lives of a future British monarch and two peers, and perhaps several hundred Rhodesian whites. The end, however, would be extremely advantageous for South Africa and would no doubt positively impact the situation in South West Africa too.

The Rhodesian contact was a Special Branch detective inspector serving out his notice prior to taking up a post with South African Military Intelligence. The team recruited to stage the assassination was a mixed bag, with at least one known Selous Scout, although quite possibly a member of the Special Branch Selous Scouts. The plan reached a reasonably advanced point before someone within the group talked. Word quickly reached Mac McGuinness who immediately passed it on to a high-level CIO operative.

The old network then kicked in. Before any official response could be mounted, word was returned to the assassination team that the plan had been exposed. The clearout was clean and expeditious and the departure swift and silent. The press and public officials all ruminated on the facts over the next few weeks but it was soon all swept aside by the global euphoria that greeted the death of white Rhodesia and birth of a new black nation. The Lancaster House agreement offered white Zimbabweans ten years of guaranteed rights to get its house in order and adapt to the new reality while black Zimbabweans had the same ten years to cool its heels before they could do whatever they wanted.

In the decade that followed, South Africa pursued a destabilization policy against Zimbabwe that drew in quite a few ex-members of the Rhodesian security forces. Among these were a number of ex-members of the Selous Scouts. For the most part, however, the regiment subsided quietly beneath the surface of history, leaving its enemies extremely cautious, its friends proud to have witnessed it all and its members grateful and privileged to have been part of it. This small brotherhood of fighting men, in existence for some six years, by the end of it all had carved its name very deeply indeed into that tablet of military history.

Notes

1. Bailey, Bill. *Hearts and Minds, Psuedo Gangs and Counter-Insurgency: Based upon Experiences from Previous Campaigns in Kenya (1952–60), Malaya (1948–60) & Rhodesia (1964–1979)*, Edith Cowan University
2. Corfield, F.D. *The Origins and Growth of the Mau Mau*, Colony and Protectorate of Kenya, 1960
3. Cilliers, J. K. *Counter-Insurgency in Rhodesia*, p223, Croom Helm, London, 1985
4. Parker, Jim. *Assignment Selous Scouts*, p27, Galago, Alberton, 2006
5. Flower, Ken. *Serving Secretly*, p115, John Murray, London, 1987
6. Parker. p29
7. Interview with Winston Hart 19/8/2011
8. Interview with Winston Hart 19/8/2011
9. Flower. p124
10. Parker. p36
11. Captain Johne Fletcher
12. Captain Johne Fletcher
13. Parker. pp36 & 37
14. Parker, p131
15. Parker. p86
16. Godwin, Peter & Hancock, Ian. *Rhodesians Never Die*, p242, Baobab, Harare, 1993
17. Reid-Daly. Lt-Col R.F., *Pamwe Chete: The Legend of the Selous Scouts*, Covos Day, Johannesburg, 2001, p480
18. Parker. p68
19. Reid-Daly. p482
20. Reid-Daly. p443
21. Flower. p252
22. Parker. p276

Peter Baxter is an author, amateur historian and African field, mountain and heritage travel guide. Born in Kenya, Peter has lived and travelled over much of southern and central Africa. He was educated in Rhodesia (Zimbabwe), leaving the country after independence for an extended bout of travel, before returning in 1989. Since then he has guided in all the major mountain ranges south of the equator, helping develop the concept of sustainable travel, and the touring of battlefield and heritage sites in East Africa. Peter lives in the United States, working on marketing African heritage travel as well as a variety of book projects. His interests include British Imperial history in Africa and the East Africa Campaign of the First World War in particular. He is married with three children.